P9-CCX-932

Student's Book

Pronunciation Pairs

An introductory course for students of English

Ann Baker • Sharon Goldstein

Fanshawe College,

London, Ontario

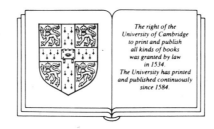

The right of the
University of Cambridge
to print and publish
all kinds of books
was granted by law
in 1534.
The University has printed
and published continuously
since 1584.

Cambridge University Press

Cambridge

New York   Port Chester

Melbourne   Sydney

1   8 90
FANSHAWE COLLEGE
STORE

$12.20

Published by the Press Syndicate of the University of Cambridge
The Pitt Building, Trumpington Street, Cambridge CB2 1RP
40 West 20th Street, New York, NY 10011, USA
10 Stamford Road, Oakleigh, Melbourne 3166, Australia

© Cambridge University Press 1990

First published 1990
Second printing 1990

Printed in the United States of America

Library of Congress Cataloging-in-Publication Data
Baker, Ann
Pronunciation pairs: an introductory course for students of English / Ann
Baker, Sharon Goldstein
p. cm.
Student's book.
1. English language – Pronunciation.   2. English language – Textbooks for
foreign speakers.   I. Goldstein, Sharon.   II. Title.
PE1137.B215   1989
428.3'4 – dc19   89–726
                                                              CIP

British Library Cataloguing in Publication Data
Baker, Ann.
Pronunciation pairs: an introductory course for students of English.
Student's book.
1. English language. Pronunciation
I. Title   II. Goldstein, Sharon
428.1

ISBN 0-521-34972-9   Student's Book
ISBN 0-521-34973-7   Teacher's Manual
ISBN 0-521-34167-1   Set of 4 Cassettes

Contents

Foreword

Pronunciation Pairs is a beginning-to-intermediate level pronunciation program, based on the innovative and highly successful British English version, *Ship or Sheep? Pronunciation Pairs* utilizes an engaging, highly visual approach for making sounds and sound processes readily discernable *and learnable*, even to beginning-level students. It provides concise explanations, both for learners and instructors, and controlled, effective practice with the vowels, consonants, word stress, and basic intonation of American English.

There is, of course, more to developing a good command of the pronunciation of a language. Students who have worked through a unit of *Pronunciation Pairs* may not yet have "mastered" the sound in question, but they will have the ability to perceive the sound more accurately and to use it in limited, controlled contexts – precisely what we expect from a supplementary pronunciation text.

The accompanying Teacher's Manual does an extraordinarily good job of providing guidance on procedures and techniques for further work, and integration of the material into more spontaneous speech. Taken as a whole, in fact, the Teacher's Manual could serve well as a reasonably comprehensive introduction to current pronunciation teaching methodology.

Pronunciation Pairs succeeds in striking a good balance between explanation and exercise; both are always clear and to the point. In addition, the accompanying cassettes are especially well done. It is the kind of program that will work well in either the classroom or the language laboratory.

William Acton
University of Houston

To the teacher

Pronunciation Pairs is designed to teach students to recognize and to produce English sounds. It also helps students learn to differentiate between sounds that they might often confuse. The basic premise is that pronunciation material should be meaningful and easily understood.

Each of the forty-six units in this book practices a different sound through a variety of activities. These include practice in both listening and speaking and moves from a highly structured practice of a sound at the word level to the practice of the sound in connected speech using more communicative activities, which include dialogues, games, puzzles, and activities for pair and group work. Stress and intonation, as well as individual sounds, are essential for communicating successfully in English, and the book introduces and practices aspects of these in almost every unit. Sections on spelling show how each sound is usually spelled in English. Throughout, the book contains illustrations that not only help students understand the material practiced but make the practice lively and interesting.

The units may be taught in whatever order seems most useful. Students may wish to work their way through the book using lessons from Section A (Vowels) and Section B (Consonants) simultaneously. Or they may prefer to choose units that are helpful for their own particular problems.

The Student's Book can be used by all students with some knowledge of English, working in class or alone. An accompanying set of four cassettes includes the practice material and examples and can be used by students working in class, in a language laboratory, or on their own. The Cassette symbol indicates material in the Student's Book recorded on the Cassettes. The Teacher's Manual provides additional help and guidance for teachers, including suggested procedures for using the practice materials in the Student's Book, activities for further practice, and suggestions for linking pronunciation with other course work.

To the student

This book has been written to help you recognize and pronounce English sounds. To make it interesting and fun to learn, there are many different types of exercises. When you do them by yourself or in class, you will realize that you are not only learning how to produce sounds: you are also practicing the skills needed to communicate in real life.

The sounds are separated into two different sections, but you do not have to work your way through the book from beginning to end. You can choose the units that practice sounds you find especially difficult, or study vowels and consonants together.

All exercises with this symbol ▱ are recorded on the Cassettes.

Section A

Vowels

VOCABULARY

First learn the words you will need in order to study how to make the sounds in this section.

YOUR MOUTH

1. This is your mouth.

2. Open your mouth.

3. Close your mouth.

4. Open your mouth a little.

5. Open your mouth a little more.

YOUR TONGUE

tongue

tongue

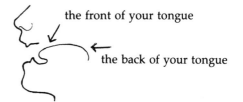

the front of your tongue

the back of your tongue

MOVING YOUR TONGUE

Put your tongue forward.

Put your tongue back.

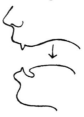

Put your tongue up.

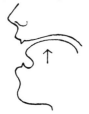

Put your tongue down.

Put your tongue forward and up.

Put your tongue down and back.

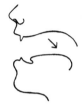

Practice iy:
easy, see, me, tea

Practice ɑ:
father, car, hot

Put your tongue up and back.

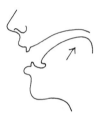

Practice uw:
who, two, school

Practice iy – ɑ – uw. Feel how your tongue moves as you say these sounds.

MUSCLES

Put your tongue forward and up.
Practice iy.

Let your tongue rest in the middle of
your mouth. Let your mouth rest open.

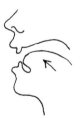

Put your hand under your chin.
Your muscles should feel tight – or tense.

Put your hand under your chin.
Relax your muscles.
Practice ʌ: cup, bus, uh

UNIT 1

iy • sheep

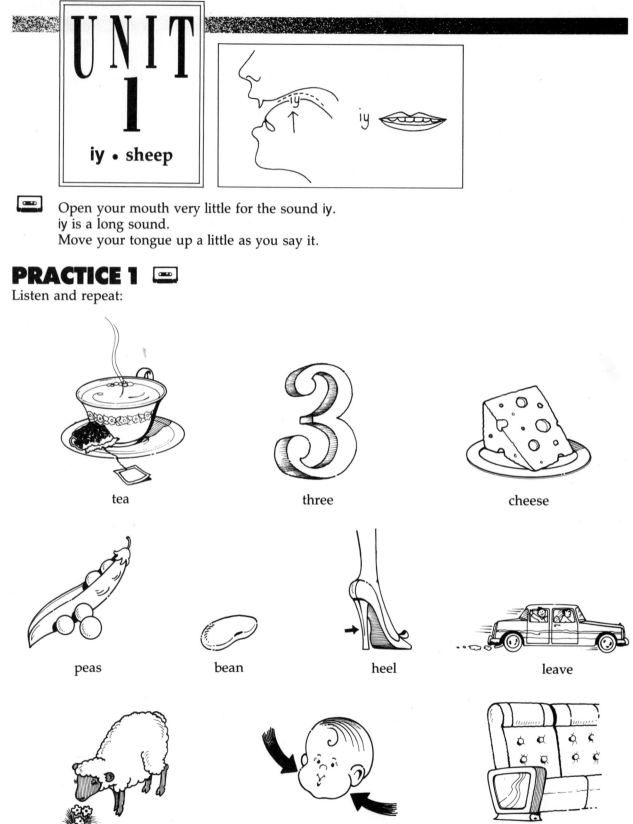

Open your mouth very little for the sound iy.
iy is a long sound.
Move your tongue up a little as you say it.

PRACTICE 1

Listen and repeat:

tea

three

cheese

peas

bean

heel

leave

sheep

cheeks

seat

PRACTICE 2

Listen and repeat:

easy	Steve	meat
see	please	roast beef
me	Peter	coffee
Lee	eat	

DIALOGUE

In a Restaurant

> **LUNCH SPECIAL**
>
> **Sandwich:**
> **Roast Beef or Cheese**
> **Coffee or Tea**
> **Only $3.15**

Peter: What are you having to eat, Lee?
Lee: I'll have a roast beef sandwich. And some tea.
Peter: Steve? Would you like a cheese sandwich or a roast beef sandwich?
Steve: A cheese sandwich. I don't eat meat.
Waitress: Yes?
Peter: We'd like one roast beef sandwich and two cheese sandwiches.
Waitress: And would you like coffee or tea?
Peter: Three teas, please.
Steve: Make that two teas. Coffee for me, please.
Waitress: (*writing down the order*) One roast beef sandwich . . . two cheese
           sandwiches . . . two teas . . . one coffee.

INTONATION

Questions with *or* Alternative questions (questions with *or*) have a rising tone on the first choice (before the *or*) and a falling tone on the last choice. The parts of words that are in blacker type are stronger, or stressed.

Would you like **coffee** or **tea**?
Would you like **beef** or **veal**?
Would you like **coffee** or **tea** or **so**da?

Now practice with somebody, using this menu (on page 6).

Example:
       Student A: Would you like bean soup or pea soup?
       Student B: Pea soup, please.

CONVERSATION

Using the menu, practice in a group of four people.
You are in a restaurant.
One person is the waiter or waitress.
The waiter/waitress asks questions: Would you like . . . or . . . ?
Give your order to the waiter/waitress.
The waiter or waitress will repeat the orders and write
    them down.

SPELLING

The sound iy is usually written with the letters *e, ee, ea,* or *ie*:

e	me, we, P<u>e</u>ter, equal, <u>e</u>ven, r<u>e</u>cent
e . . . e	these, complete, scene, extreme, Steve
ee	see, three, thirteen, beef, sheep, street, feel coffee, cheese, sleeve, freeze
ea	tea, eat, meal, cheap, speak, repeat, teacher easy, mean, please, leave, peace
ie	chief, belief, field, movie, cookie piece, believe, niece

Other spellings:

y	easy, only, very, ready, many, funny, happy, crazy
ey	key, money, monkey, donkey
ei	receive, ceiling, either,* neither*
i	taxi, ski, visa
i . . . e	machine, police, magazine
eo	people

*Some people say these words with the sound **ay**.

MENU
Today's Specials
SOUP:
Bean Soup or Pea Soup
MEAT:
Roast Beef or Veal
VEGETABLE:
Beans or Peas or Beets
DESSERT:
Cheesecake or Ice Cream
or Peaches
Coffee or Tea

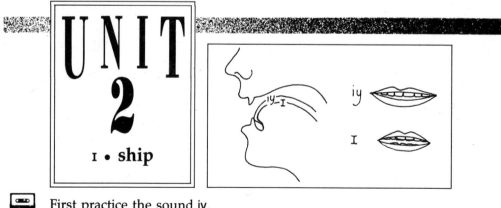

UNIT 2
ɪ • ship

First practice the sound iy.
Then open your mouth a *little* more.
iy is a long sound.
ɪ is a shorter and more relaxed sound.

PRACTICE 1

Listen and repeat:

	Sound 1	_Sound 2_	
	sheep	ship	
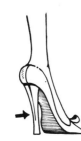	heel	hill	
	seat	sit	
	cheeks	chicks	
	feel	fill	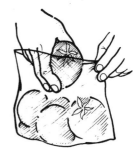

7

TEST 🔲

Listen to these sentences. Circle the word in parentheses that you hear in each sentence.

1. He wants to buy a (sheep/ship).
2. Those (heels/hills) are very high.
3. Look at those (cheeks/chicks).
4. Did you (feel/fill) the glass?
5. He isn't going to (leave/live).

PRACTICE 2 🔲

Listen and repeat:

is	Lynn	with	sixty
it's	Bill	film	fifty
isn't	Mrs. Kim	interesting	beginning
kid	Jim	minutes	quick

DIALOGUE 🔲

An Interesting Film

Mrs. Kim:	Hello, Bill. Hello, Lynn.
Bill:	Hi, Mrs. Kim. Is Jim in?
Lynn:	Is he coming with us to the film?
Mrs. Kim:	Oh, Jim's sick.
Bill:	Here he is! Hi, Jim.
Lynn:	Are you sick, Jim?
Jim:	Is it an interesting film?
Lynn:	It's *Billy the Kid*.
Bill:	And it begins in six minutes.
Mrs. Kim:	Jim, if you're sick . . .
Jim:	Quick! Or we'll miss the beginning of the film!

STRESS 🔲

Numbers   Listen and repeat:

three	thir**teen**	**thir**ty	3	13	30
four	four**teen**	**for**ty	4	14	40
five	fif**teen**	**fif**ty	5	15	50
six	six**teen**	**six**ty	6	16	60
seven	seven**teen**	**sev**enty	7	17	70
eight	eigh**teen**	**eigh**ty	8	18	80
nine	nine**teen**	**nine**ty	9	19	90

GAME

Mini-Bingo

Play in a group of about five people.
One person calls out the numbers above in any order.
The others each choose one of the boxes A, B, C, or D below.
Cross out each number in your box as it is called (or put a small piece of paper on top of each number as it is called).
The first person to cross out all the numbers in one box wins.

A

13	3	80
7	19	50
17	90	8

B

60	4	16
20	30	13
70	5	90

C

5	15	16
70	90	3
40	7	18

D

60	6	15
8	14	17
9	90	80

SPELLING

The sound ɪ is usually written with the letter *i* or (less often) with the letter *y*.

- *i*   ship, did, win, six, fifteen, interesting, picture, fill, sick, quick, miss, film, listen, little, different
     big – biggest, swim – swimmer, begin – beginning
     minute, city, finish, give, live
- *y*   syllable, system, sympathy, rhythm, mystery, physics, gym

Other spellings:

- *e, ee*   English, pretty, been
- *ui*   build, building, guitar
- *u*   busy, business
- *o*   women

UNIT 3

ε • yes

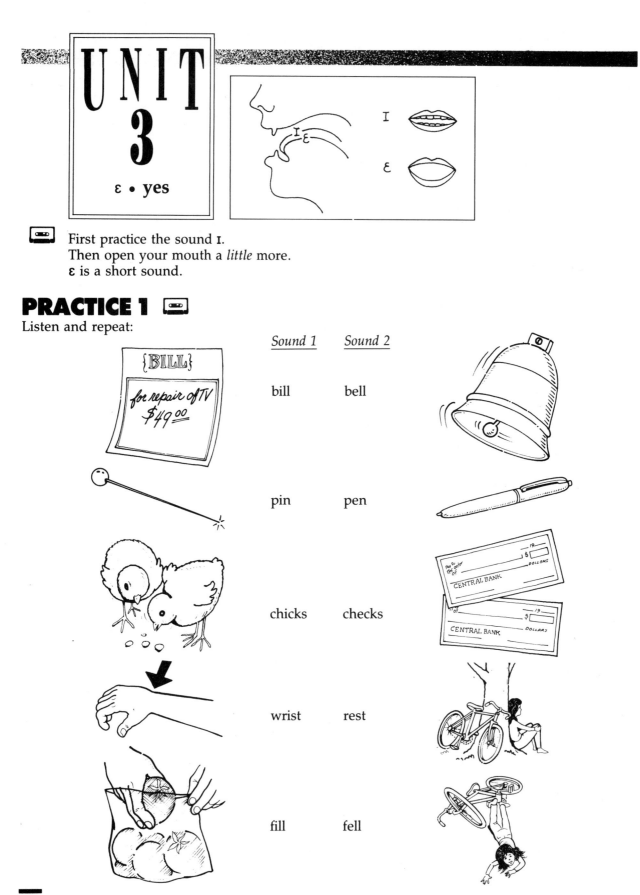

First practice the sound ɪ.
Then open your mouth a *little* more.
ε is a short sound.

PRACTICE 1 🔲

Listen and repeat:

Sound 1	Sound 2
bill	bell
pin	pen
chicks	checks
wrist	rest
fill	fell

TEST

Listen to these sentences. Circle the word in parentheses that you hear in each sentence.

1. You dropped a (pin/pen).
2. Did you get the (bill/bell)?
3. This coffee tastes (bitter/better).
4. Her name is (Ginny/Jenny).
5. Whose (chicks/checks) are these?

PRACTICE 2 ▭

Listen and repeat:

left	Jenny	ten cents
Fred	Ellen	any
spend	help yourself	everybody
friend	Venice	everything
shelf	jealous	expensive

DIALOGUE ▭

An Expensive Vacation

Ed:	Hi, Ellen! Hi, Fred! Hi, Jenny!
Fred:	Hi, Ed. Cigarette?
Ed:	No, thanks, Fred.
Ellen:	Help yourself to a drink.
Jenny:	Look on the shelf to your left.
Fred:	How did you spend your vacation, Ed?
Ed:	I went to Venice with a friend.
Everybody:	Well!
Ellen:	We're all jealous.
Fred:	Was it expensive?
Ed:	Yes. Very. I spent everything I had.
Jenny:	Don't you have any money left?
Ed:	Yes, Jenny. Ten cents!

INTONATION ▭

Statements usually have a *falling* tone at the end.
Wh-questions (Who? What? Why? When? Where? How?) also usually have a *falling* tone at the end.
Yes/No questions (questions you can answer with "yes" or "no") usually have a *rising* tone at the end.

Examples:

Wh-question:	**How** did you **spend** your va**ca**tion?
Statement:	I **went** to **Ven**ice.
Yes/No question:	Was it ex**pen**sive?
Statement:	**Yes. Ve**ry.

11

CONVERSATION

Practice this conversation. Use the place names below.

> How did you spend your vacation?
> I went to . . .
> Was it expensive?
> Yes. Very.   *or*   No. Not very.

Mexico   **Ven**ice   **Bel**gium   **Den**mark   **South** A**mer**ica   **Tex**as
Quebec   **Vi**enna   The **Neth**erlands   **Ec**uador   **Len**ingrad

SPELLING

The sound ɛ is usually written with the letter *e*:

> *e*   yes, pen, check, went, left, spend, best, yourself, exp̱ensive, ḇetter, tennis, correct
> get – getting, red – redder
> s̱even, ev̱ery, ṯelephone, special, ṉecessary

Other spellings:

> *ea*   jealous, bread, breakfast, heavy, weather, head, already, dead, health, measure, pleasant, read (past tense)
> *a*   any, anyone, many
> *ai*   said, again
> *ay*   says
> *ie*   friend

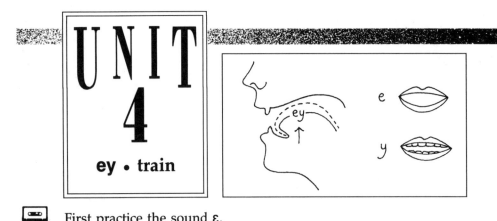

First practice the sound ɛ.
Close your mouth *very* little.
ey is a long sound. Move your tongue up a little as you say it.
The **e** part is long. The **y** part is very short.

PRACTICE 1 📼

Listen and repeat:

		Sound 1	_Sound 2_	
		pen	pain	
		wet	wait	
		tell	tail	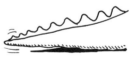
		test	taste	
		pepper	paper	

TEST 📼

Listen to these sentences. Circle the word in parentheses that you hear.

1. Can I have some more (pepper/paper)?
2. This (pen/pain) is terrible.
3. I want to (sell/sail) the boat.
4. (Test/Taste) the cake and see if it's done.
5. Put it in the (shed/shade).

PRACTICE 2 📼

Listen and repeat:

Hey!	away	waiting	8:18
say	mistake	station	Plainview
they	made	late	8:08
Mr. Gray	afraid	ages	changed
today	train	April	eighth

DIALOGUE 📼

At the Train Station

(Mr. Gray is waiting at the station for a train.)

Mr. Gray: Hey! This train's late! I've been waiting here for ages.
Conductor: Which train are you waiting for?
Mr. Gray: The 8:18 to Plainview.
Conductor: The 8:18? I'm afraid you've made a mistake, sir.
Mr. Gray: A mistake? But I take this train every day. And that's what my schedule says: Plainview 8:18.
Conductor: Oh, no, sir. The Plainview train leaves at 8:08.
Mr. Gray: At 8:08?
Conductor: That's right. They changed the schedule at the end of April. Today's the eighth of May.
Mr. Gray: Changed it? I guess they changed it while I was away on vacation. Can I see the new schedule? Where does it say that?
Conductor: Right here. Train to Plainview 8:08.
Mr. Gray: Hm! So the train isn't late. I'm late.

INTONATION 📼

Surprise

A: Mr. Gray takes the train to Plainview at 8:18 every day.
B: At 8:18?
C: To **Plainview**?
D: Mr. **Gray**?
E: **Every day**?

In this conversation, B, C, D, and E are all surprised by what A says. B is surprised that he takes the train <u>at 8:18.</u> C is surprised that he takes the train <u>to Plainview.</u> D is surprised that it's <u>Mr. Gray</u> who takes the train. E is surprised that he takes the train <u>every day.</u>

Listen and repeat:

The **eighth**?

To**day**?

Going a**way**?

By **plane**?

CONVERSATION 🔲

Practice in pairs. B should sound surprised about the underlined part of the sentence.

Example:

It's <u>the eighth</u> of April.
Student A: It's the eighth of April.
Student B: The eighth?

1. It's <u>the eighth</u> of May.

2. Yes. It's Mrs. Gray's birthday <u>today</u>.

3. Yes. She's <u>eighty-eight</u> years old.

4. Yes. And she's <u>going away</u> on vacation.

5. That's right. She's going <u>by plane</u>.

6. Well, I guess it might be dangerous at her age, but she wants to go <u>to Spain</u>.

7. Yes. Why don't <u>you</u> go with her?

SPELLING

The sound **ey** is usually written with the letters *a, a . . . e, ai,* or *ay.*

a	baby, later, paper, April, station, vacation, famous, table, dangerous
a . . . e	late, page, same, name, age, take, mistake, plane, made, place, change, taste
ai	train, pain, wait, tail, afraid, Spain, rain, remain, paint raise, praise
ay	day, say, gray, stay, away, today, birthday, May, maybe

Other spellings:

eigh	eight, eighteen, eighty-eight, eighth, weigh, weight, neighbor
aigh	straight
ea	great, break, steak
ey	they, hey, obey
ei	veil, vein

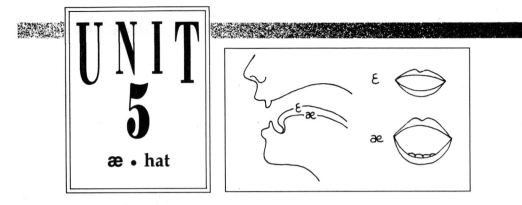

UNIT 5
æ • hat

First practice the sound ɛ.
Then open your mouth a *little* more.

PRACTICE 1

Listen and repeat:

	Sound 1	Sound 2	
	X	axe	
	pen	pan	
	men	man	
	said	sad	
	beg	bag	

TEST 🔲

Listen to these sentences. Circle the word in parentheses that you hear.

1. Did you see the (men/man)?
2. Is this (pen/pan) new?
3. Everyone (left/laughed) when I said that.
4. They are (said/sad) to be leaving.
5. Is that man in the picture (dead/Dad)?

PRACTICE 2 🔲

Listen and repeat:

bank	cash	Saturday	exactly
catch	ma'am	manager	afternoon
that's	Alice	photograph	plaid pants
man	happened	moustache	black jacket
glasses	handful	absolutely	plastic bag
past	grabbed		

DIALOGUE 🔲

The Bank Robber

(*Alice is a teller in a bank.*)

Detective: Excuse me, ma'am, have you ever seen the man in this photograph?

Alice: Yes! That's him! That's the man who robbed the bank! But he had a moustache.

Detective: A moustache! This man? Last Saturday?

Alice: Yes. He was wearing plaid pants and a black jacket. And he had on very dark glasses.

Detective: Can you tell me exactly what happened?

Alice: Well, I was working at the bank Saturday afternoon. Suddenly, this man ran past me, grabbed a handful of cash, and stuffed it in a plastic bag.

Detective: And what happened after that?

Alice: He ran back out again. It all happened so fast. The manager ran after him, but he couldn't catch him. The man was running too fast.

Detective: And you're absolutely sure the man in the photograph is the same man?

Alice: Yes. Absolutely. That's him.

Detective: Thank you for your help.

Alice: I hope you catch him!

SENTENCE STRESS 📼

In English, the important words in a sentence (usually nouns, verbs, adjectives, and adverbs) are stressed. The unimportant words (usually words like *the, and, is, it*) are not stressed. Normally, the last important word in the sentence has the most stress. Listen and repeat:

> That's the **per**son who **robbed** the **bank**!
>
> Do you **mean** the **man** with the **black pants?**
>
> **No.** The **wom**an with the **plas**tic **bag**.

CONVERSATION

Practice this conversation about the people in the pictures.

Example:

A: That's the person who robbed the bank!
B: Do you mean the man with the black pants?
A: No. The woman with the plastic bag.

black pants

red hat

plaid jacket

plastic bag

mask

moustache

backpack

dark glasses

SPELLING

The sound æ is almost always written with the letter *a*:

    a   hat, bank, jacket, example, plastic, glasses, happen
        sad – sadder, fat – fattest, grab – grabbed
        taxi, manager, family, camera, mechanic, natural, travel, have

Other spellings:

    au   laugh, aunt*
    ai   plaid

*Some people say *aunt* with the sound ɑ.

18

UNIT 6
Review

LISTENING PRACTICE

1: iy	*2: ɪ*	*3: ey*	*4: ɛ*	*5: æ*
lead	lid	laid	led	lad
beat	bit	bait	bet	bat
seal	sill	sail	sell	Sal
dean	din	Dane	den	Dan

When you hear one of the words above, give the number for its sound.

Example 1:   Dane
        [sound] 3

Example 2:   bat
        [sound] 5

PRONUNCIATION PRACTICE

Listen and repeat:

eat 6	dinner 8	made 13	lemon 1	mat 2
seat 12	sit 3	steak 5	ready 10	grass 9
tea 7	chicken	great 15	bread 14	salad 4
				backyard 16

DIALOGUE

Dinner on the Grass

Ben: Is dinner ready?
Ann: Yes. Let's eat in the backyard.
Ben: Shall we sit on this seat?
Ann: Let's sit on this mat on the grass.
Ben: Are we having chicken?
Ann: No. I made steak and salad.
Ben: Great! Is there any bread?
Ann: Yes. And lemon cake and tea.

JUMBLED SPELLINGS

Unscramble these words. (Hint: They are all names for parts of the body.) Write one letter in each square. Use all the letters. The letters in the circles form a new jumbled word. This word completes the sentence at the end.

Example:

TEFE F E E T

1. DAHN   H A N D

2. PIL   L I P

3. ETHET   T E E T H

4. CAEF   F A C E

5. THECS   C H E S T

If you have a problem with your (WORD #3), you see a ⬚⬚⬚⬚⬚⬚⬚

Which vowel sound does each word (1–5) have? Make sure you say each word with a different vowel sound.

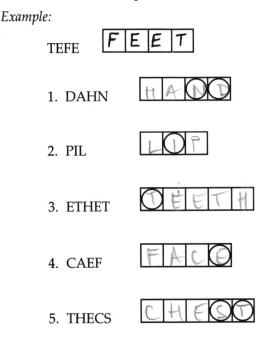

UNIT
7
Λ • cup

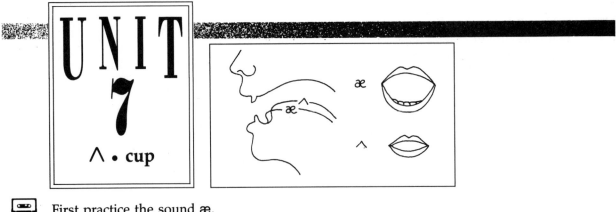

First practice the sound æ.
Then put your tongue up and back a little. Close your mouth a little.
Your tongue should rest in the middle of your mouth.
ʌ is a short, relaxed sound.

PRACTICE 1 📼

Listen and repeat:

Sound 1	_Sound 2_
cap	cup
bag	bug
sack	suck
ban	bun
rag	rug

TEST 🔲

Listen to these sentences. Circle the word in parentheses that you hear.

1. There's a big (bag/bug) on the table.
2. This (cap/cup) is too small.
3. I threw away the old (rag/rug).
4. They (ran/run) quickly.
5. What happened to your (ankle/uncle)?

PRACTICE 2 🔲

Listen and repeat:

unhappy	nothing	shut up
uninteresting	cousin	dumb
understand	honey	just once
love	Sunny	month
much	Russ	company
lunch	fun	wonderful

DIALOGUE 🔲

Love

Russ: Honey, why are you so unhappy?
Janet: (*Janet says nothing.*)
Russ: Honey, why are you so sad? I don't understand.
Janet: You don't love me, Russ!
Russ: But honey, I love you very much.
Janet: No, you don't. You're in love with my cousin, Sunny. You think she's smart and fun to be with and you think I'm dumb and uninteresting.
Russ: Janet, just once last month I went out to lunch with Sunny. There's nothing for you to be jealous about. I like your company much better than Sunny's.
Janet: Oh, shut up, Russ.
Russ: But honey, I think you're wonderful. There's nothing . . .
Janet: Oh, SHUT UP!

INTONATION 🔲

Making a List   Listen and repeat:

He bought a c͡up and some n͡uts.
He bought a c͡up, some n͡uts, and some h͡oney.
He bought a c͡up, some n͡uts, some h͡oney, and a br͡ush.

GAME

"My Uncle Went to London"

Practice this game first in groups of five or six people and then with the whole class.
Choose any words from the list below – or add your own words with the sound ʌ.

Example:

    Student A: My uncle went to London and he spent a lot of money. He
                 bought a bus.
    Student B: My uncle went to London and he spent a lot of money. He
                 bought a bus and a dozen cups.

Each student adds something to the list. You must remember what the other students
have said.
Practice saying the words before you start:

a **rug**	· some **butter**
. a **bus**	some **won**derful **honey**
· a **trum**pet	' some **on**ions
a **trunk**	a **cou**ple of **brush**es
. a **truck**	a **rub**ber **duck**
· a **dozen cups**	· some **gum**
· some **nuts**	. a **mon**key
· a **hun**dred **but**tons	· some **funny sun**glasses
some **com**fortable **gloves**	· a **set** of **drums**

SPELLING

The sound ʌ is usually written with the letters *u* or *o*.

    u   bus, cup, much, under, lunch, husband, funny, button, rubber
          cut – cutting, run – runner, running, sun – sunny
          study
    o   wonderful, nothing, month, mother, son, once, color, other, money, love,
          something, done, none, come, cover, government

Other spellings:

    ou   country, cousin, young, enough, touch, trouble, couple
    oo   blood, flood
    oe   does, doesn't

UNIT 8

Part 1
ə • a banana

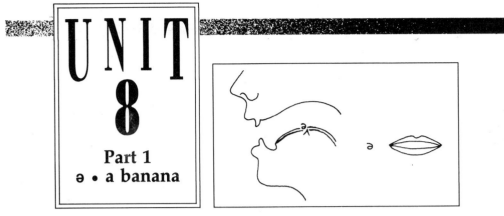

First practice the sound ʌ.
Then make it very short. This is ə.
ə is a very short sound. It is always unstressed.

We use the sound ə in many words and syllables that are not important and not stressed. In this lesson, vowels pronounced as ə have a dot under them.

PRACTICE 1

Listen and repeat:

baṇanạs

tọmatoes

ạ **problẹm**

ạ **ques**tiọn

ạn **oniọn**

sọme **choc**ỏlạte

excẹllẹnt

terrịble

PRACTICE 2

Listen and repeat:

1.

ạ cup ọf coffee

2.

_____

3.

ạ can ọf Coke

4.

_____

5.

ạ pound ọf tomatoes

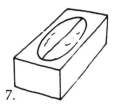

6.

_____

7.

ạ box ọf tissues

8.

_____

PRACTICE 3

Listen and repeat:

She cạn ride ạ bike.   She can't drive ạ car.

She cạn play thẹ guitar.   She can't play thẹ piano.

She cạn sail ạ boat.   She can't swim.

Cạn she ride ạ bike?   Yes, she can.

Cạn she drive ạ car?   No, she can't.

TEST 🔲

Listen to these sentences. Circle the word in parentheses that you hear.

1. He (can't/can) play the piano.
2. I (can't/can) stand on my head.
3. (Can't/Can) you help me?
4. He (can't/can) speak Spanish, but his sister (can't/can).
5. I (can't/can) meet you tomorrow.

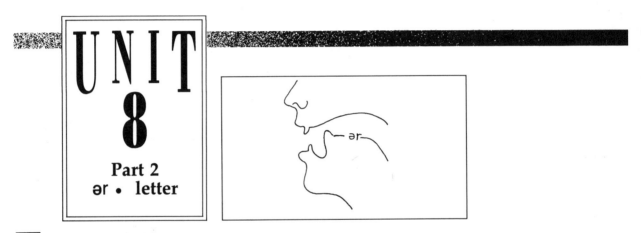

UNIT 8
Part 2
ər • letter

🔲 First practice ə.
Now curl the tip of your tongue up and back a little as you say ə.
ər is pronounced together as one sound.

PRACTICE 4 🔲

Listen and repeat:

painter	butcher	tailor	cab driver
actor	barber	carpenter	bank teller
singer	doctor	reporter	police officer
waiter	lawyer	designer	computer programmer
			picture

Talk about the pictures.

Example: PICTURE 1
    A: **What** does she **do**?
    B: She's a **painter**.

1   2   3   4

5   6   7   8

DIALOGUE 🔲

Asking a Favor

A: I'm going to the | doctor.
                  | cleaner's.

B: Can you get something for me at the | supermarket?
                                         | drugstore?

A: But the | supermarket   is a | long way   from the | doctor.
           | drugstore | mile | cleaner's.

B: No. Not *that* | supermarket.   Not the one that's next to the
                  | drugstore.

| movie theater.   I mean the one that's near the | butcher.
| record store. | barber.

A: Oh, that one. Well, what do you want me to get?

B: Some | bread   and a | can of tuna fish   and an | onion.
          | aspirin | box of tissues | address book.

SPELLING

The sound ə can be written with any vowel letter.

a about, across, <u>a</u>partment, another, b<u>a</u>nan<u>a</u>, dialogue, woman, sofa, chocolate
     sugar, popular, liar

e problem, open, quiet, apartment, tel<u>e</u>phone, kitchen, exc<u>e</u>ll<u>e</u>nt
     answer, lawyer, writer, another, father, mother, lett<u>e</u>r

i possible, terrible, medicine, sim<u>i</u>lar, animal, notice, service, promise

o today, police, compare, second, comm<u>o</u>n, question, opinion, welcome,
     handsome, purpose
     doct<u>o</u>r, tailor, calculator, visitor, col<u>o</u>r

u upon, suggest, support, success, circus, aut<u>u</u>mn, lettuce
     picture, survive, fut<u>u</u>re

Other spellings:

ou famous, nervous

y anonymous

UNIT 9

ɑ • father

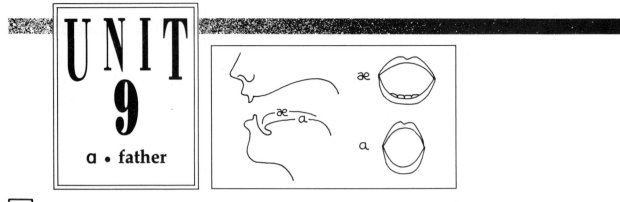

 Put your tongue down and back: ɑ.

PRACTICE 1

Listen and repeat:

	Sound 1	Sound 2	
	hat	hot	
	cat	cot	
	cap	cop	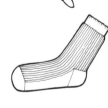
	sack	sock	
	ran	Ron	

28

PRACTICE 2 📼
Listen and repeat:

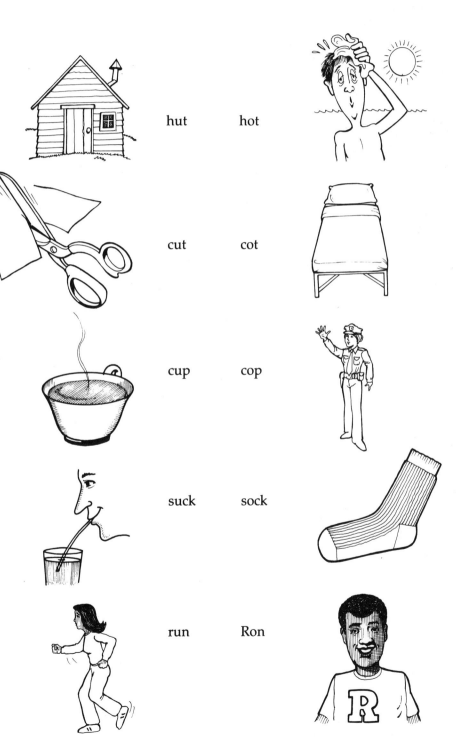

	Sound 1	*Sound 2*	
	hut	hot	
	cut	cot	
	cup	cop	
	suck	sock	
	run	Ron	

TEST ▭

Listen to these sentences. Circle the word in parentheses that you hear.

1. He keeps his money in a (sack/sock).
2. Don't sit on the (cat/cot)!
3. Did you see that (cap/cup/cop)?
4. I put the (map/mop) away.
5. That (color/collar) looks good on you.
6. There's a (duck/dock) on the lake.

PRACTICE 3 ▭

Listen and repeat:

job	socks	bottle	marvelous
hot	shop	Mr. Block	horrible
not	modern	hard	wash
lots	popular	star	want

DIALOGUE ▭

TV Commercial for "Starwash"

Voice A:	What's the matter, Mr. Block?
Mr. Block:	What's the matter? I want a break from this horrible job of washing socks!
Voice B:	Buy a bottle of Starwash, Mr. Block.
Voice C:	Starwash does the job.
Voice D:	But it's not a hard job with Starwash.
Voice A:	You don't need lots of hot water with Starwash.
Voice B:	Start washing the modern way – with Starwash.
Voice C:	Starwash is marvelous for all your washable clothes.
Everybody:	Starwash is so popular!
Voice C:	Next time you shop, pick up a bottle of Starwash.

INTONATION ▭

Listen and repeat:

What a **hard job**!

What a **fast car**!

What a **won**derful **car**pet!

CONVERSATION

Practice this conversation about the pictures below.

A: Look at that car!
B: What a fast car!

Use any of these words:

large	**fun**ny
dark	**ug**ly
marvelous	**won**derful
fast	fan**tas**tic

bottle

box

carpet

clock

car

sock

SPELLING

The sound ɑ is usually written with the letter *o* or *a*.

o stop, shop, job, d<u>o</u>ctor, clock, bottle, college, problem, possible
shop – shopping, stop – stopped, hot – hotter
popular, modern, promise, copy, body, operate
horrible,* sorry,* tomorrow,* borrow,* orange,* doll,* fog,* jog*

a father, star, large, garden, hard, carpet, aren't, palm, calm
wash,* want,* watch,* wallet,* Washington,* quality,* quantity*

Other spellings:

ow   knowledge
ea, e (before *r*) heart, sergeant

*Some people say these words with the sound ɔ instead of ɑ.

31

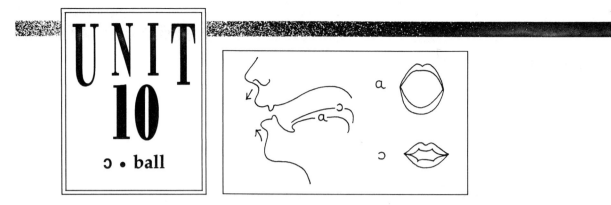

UNIT 10

ɔ • ball

First practice the sound ɑ.
Then put your tongue up and back a little and move your lips forward a little.

PRACTICE 1

Listen and repeat:

Sound 1	Sound 2
Don	Dawn
cot	caught
card	cord
far	four
part	port

PRACTICE 2 📼

Listen and repeat:

	Sound 1	*Sound 2*	
	cut	caught	
	dug	dog	
	cuff	cough	
	bus	boss	
	lung	long	

33

TEST

Listen to these sentences. Circle the word in parentheses that you hear.

1. This is my friend (Don/Dawn).
2. Is it (far/four)?
3. I need a new (card/cord).
4. I'm waiting for the (bus/boss).
5. She (cut/caught) the piece of paper.
6. Did you see the (collar/color/caller)?

PRACTICE 3

Listen and repeat:

all	sports	awful	always
lost	morning	audience	toward
thought	airport	walking	Paul Short
fault	reporter	falling	George Small

A Football Game

DIALOGUE

A Football Game   Sports Report on Channel 4

Announcer: This morning the Horses returned from their game in Boston. Paul Short, our sports reporter, was at the airport to meet them.

Paul Short: Good morning. I'm Paul Short. All the football players are walking toward me. Here's George Small, the halfback. Good morning, George.

George Small: Good morning. Are you a reporter?

Paul Short: Yes. I'm from Channel 4. Please tell our audience what you thought about the game in Boston.

George Small: Well, it was just awful. We lost. The score was 4 to 44. But it wasn't my fault.

Paul Short: Whose fault was it?

George Small: The quarterback's.

Paul Short: The quarterback's?

George Small: Yes. The quarterback's. He was always falling down or dropping the ball!

STRESS AND INTONATION 📼

Listen and repeat:

A: George played baseball in **Bos**ton.

B: **Rea**lly? I thought George played **foot**ball in Boston.

A: George played football in New **York.**

B: **Rea**lly? I thought George played football in **Bos**ton.

A: Paul played football in **Bos**ton.

B: **Rea**lly? I thought **George** played football in Boston.

In these conversations, B is surprised by something that A says. In B's responses, the main stress and intonation change is on the information that is *different* from what A said.

CONVERSATION

B is surprised by something A says. B should be sure to put the main stress and intonation change in the right place. Work in pairs. Then change roles.

Example:

A: The football player's name was **Paul.**

B: **Rea**lly? I thought the re**por**ter's name was Paul.

1. A: The score was 8 to 44.
   B: Really? I thought the score was 4 to 44.

2. A: Boston lost the game.
   B: Really? I thought New York lost the game.

3. A: George Small played football in the evening.
   B: Really? I thought he played football in the morning.

4. A: George talked to Dawn at the airport.
   B: Really? I thought he talked to Paul at the airport.

5. A: It wasn't George's fault.
   B: Really? I thought it was George's fault.

SPELLING

The sound ɔ is usually written with the letters *o*, *a*, *au*, or *aw*.

o   dog, long, wrong, boss, office, lost, across, morning, sports, corner, short, more, before, score, tore, bored

a   (especially before *l*) tall, call, fall, always, already, also, football, walk,* talk,* water, warm, quarter

au fault, audience, August, because

aw saw, awful, law, draw, dawn

Other spellings:

augh caught, taught, daughter

ough thought, bought, fought

ou(r) four, your, pour, of course

oo(r) door, floor

oa broad

*The *l* in these words is silent. Some people say ɑ instead of ɔ in many of these words.

UNIT 11

ow · no

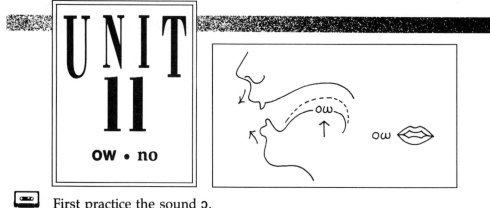

First practice the sound ɔ.
Then put the back of your tongue up a little.
As you say this sound, put your lips forward into a circle.
ow is a long sound, with two parts. The **w** part is very short.

PRACTICE 1

Listen and repeat:

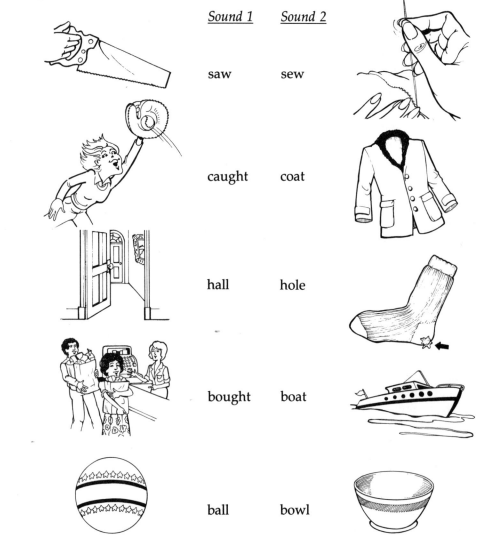

Sound 1	Sound 2
saw	sew
caught	coat
hall	hole
bought	boat
ball	bowl

TEST 📼

Listen to these sentences. Circle the word in parentheses that you hear.

1. I fell in the (hall/hole).
2. Could you (saw/sew) this for me?
3. Don't drop the (ball/bowl)!
4. I (walk/woke) early in the morning.
5. Were you (called/cold)?

PRACTICE 2 📼

Listen and repeat:

Oh!	throw	don't	joking
no	snow	Joan	woke
ago	over	groans	coat
window	open	closed	October
hello	Joe Como	OK	

DIALOGUE 📼

Snow in October

(*Joe Como is sleeping, but Joan woke up a few minutes ago.*)

Joan: Joe! Joe! JOE! Hello?
Joe: (*groans*) Oh, no. What's the matter, Joan?
Joan: Look out the window.
Joe: No. My eyes are closed and I'm going back to sleep.
Joan: Don't go to sleep, Joe. Come look at the snow.
Joe: Snow? But it's only October. I know there's no snow.
Joan: Come over to the window.
Joe: Stop joking, Joan. There's no snow.
Joan: OK. I'm going to put on my coat and go out and make a snowball and throw it at you. Then you'll open your eyes, Joe Como!

PRACTICE 3 📼

Rhyming Words   Some of these words have the sound **ow**. Listen and repeat.

phone	come	throw
done	home	know
snow	groan	some
now	one	

Which words in the list rhyme with:

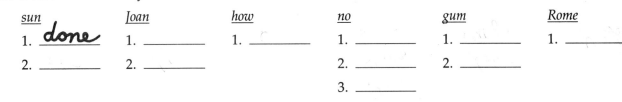

sun	*Joan*	*how*	*no*	*gum*	*Rome*
1. *done*	1. _____	1. _____	1. _____	1. _____	1. _____
2. _____	2. _____		2. _____	2. _____	
			3. _____		

Rhyming Crossword

The answers are words that rhyme with the clues but do not have the same meaning.

Clues

Across:	**Down:**
1 only	1 show
3 don't	2 Jell-O
6 know	4 John
7 Joe	5 snow
8 willow	7 no

SPELLING

The sound **ow** is usually written with the letters *o, o . . . e, oa,* or *ow.*

o	go, hello, no, open, over, joking, Oct**o**ber, ago
	old, older, sold, told, roll, most, don't, won't, only, both
o . . . e	home, hole, nose, phone, those, joke, woke, wrote
oa	boat, coat, road, Joan, soap, coast
ow	know, show, snow, throw, slow, window, yellow, tomorrow

Other spellings:

oe	toe, Joe
ough	though, dough
ew	sew
oh	oh!

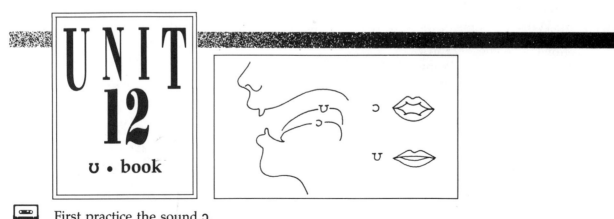

UNIT 12

ʊ • book

First practice the sound ɔ.
Then put the back of your tongue up a little and close your mouth a little.
ʊ is a short, relaxed sound.

PRACTICE 1

Listen and repeat:

	Sound 1	*Sound 2*	
	fall	full	
	talk	took	
	ball	bull	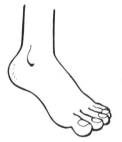
	fought	foot	
	Paul	pull	

39

TEST 🔲

Listen to these sentences. Circle the word in parentheses that you hear.

1. They (talk/took) too much.
2. Watch out for the (ball/bull)!
3. This (wall/wool) is dirty.
4. It was (fall/full) then.
5. (Paul/Pull), don't push the door.

PRACTICE 2 🔲

Listen and repeat:

put	cook	football	couldn't
look	full	bookshelf	shouldn't
foot	good	cookbooks	bedroom
took	woods	cushions	living room

DIALOGUE 🔲

The Lost Book

Mr. Cook:	Paula Cook! Could you tell me where you put my book?
Mrs. Cook:	Which book? Your football book?
Mr. Cook:	No. *A Walk in the Woods.*
Mrs. Cook:	Isn't it on the bookshelf?
Mr. Cook:	No. The bookshelf is full of cookbooks.
Mrs. Cook:	Then shouldn't you look in the bedroom?
Mr. Cook:	I've looked there. I'm sure you took that book and put it somewhere.
Mrs. Cook:	I didn't put it anywhere. Look in the living room.
Mr. Cook:	I've looked.
Mrs. Cook:	All over? Under the sofa cushions?
Mr. Cook:	Couldn't you at least help me look for it?
Mrs. Cook:	Look. It's on the floor near your foot.
Mr. Cook:	Ah! Good!

NEGATIVE QUESTIONS 🔲

Listen and repeat:

shouldn't he?   **could**n't we?   **would**n't you?

Shouldn't he look near his foot?
Couldn't we walk through the woods?

Practice in pairs:

Example:
A: ___*Couldn't we*___ walk through the woods?
B: Yes, we could.

1. A: _____ push the door?
   B: Yes, he should.

2. A: _____ this coat look good on Mrs. Cook?
   B: Yes, it would.

3. A: _____ buy some more bookshelves?
   B: Yes, we should.

4. A: _____ put some sugar in the cookies?
   B: Yes, she should.

5. A: _____ like to look at this book?
   B: Yes, I would.

SPELLING

The sound ʊ is usually written with the letters *oo* or *u*.

  oo good, wood, stood, look, took, foot, cookbook, wool
        room,* bedroom,* roof,* root*

  u   full, pull, push, put, sugar, cushion

Other spellings:

  ou could, would, should

  o   woman, wolf

*Many people pronounce these words with the sound uw.

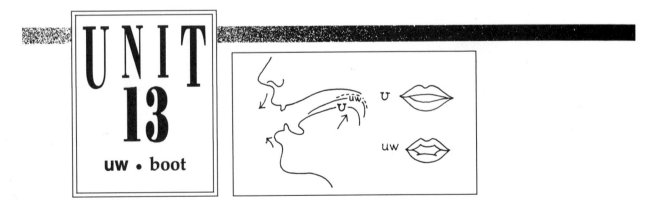

First practice the sound ʊ.
ʊ is a short sound.
Now put your tongue up and back. Push your lips forward into a circle.
uw is a long sound.
Push your lips into a tighter circle as you say it.

PRACTICE 1

Listen and repeat:

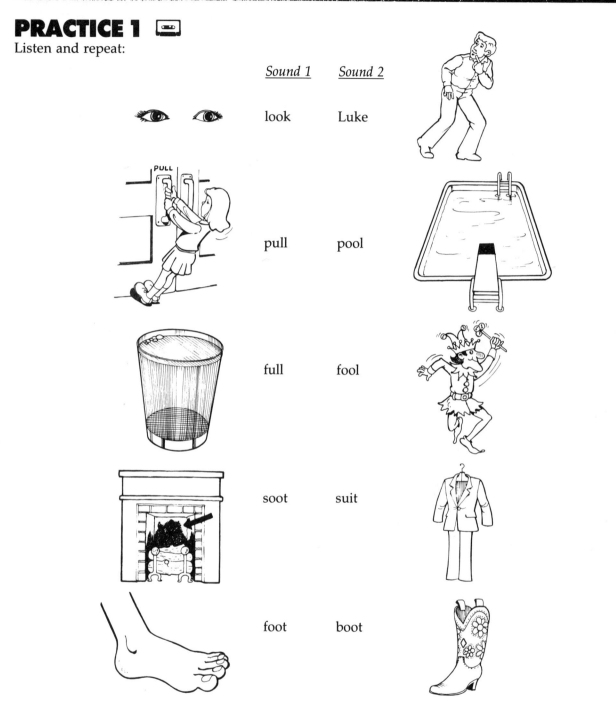

	Sound 1	Sound 2
	look	Luke
	pull	pool
	full	fool
	soot	suit
	foot	boot

TEST

Listen to these sentences. Circle the word in parentheses that you hear.

1. The sign on the door says ("Pull"/"Pool").

2. (Look/Luke), I want you to come here.

3. Where did that black (soot/suit) come from?

PRACTICE 2

Listen and repeat:

do	Sue	Tuesday	newspaper
you, too	Peru	student	music
soon	Lou	introduce	Happy New Year
shoes	blue		

DIALOGUE

A New Year's Eve Party

STRESS

Listen and repeat:

A: Do you like this music?
B: Yes. Do you?

A: What do you do?
B: I'm a student. What do you do? *or* What about you?

CONVERSATION

Work in pairs. Make up a question for A in the conversations below. Use ideas from the conversations at the New Year's Eve party above or your own ideas.

Example:

A: *Happy New Year!*
B: Happy New Year to you, too.

1. A:
   B: Thank you. It's new.

2. A:
   B: Really? Me too.

3. A:
   B: Nice to meet you, too.

4. A:
   B: Nice to meet you.

5. A:
   B: Yes. Do you?

6. A:
   B: I'm a student. What about you?

7. A:
   B: Yes. What do *you* do?

SPELLING

The sound **uw** is usually written with the letters *oo* or *u*.

oo	afternoon, food, school, pool, soon, moon, spoon, boot, smooth, too room,* root,* roof*
oo . . . e	choose, loose
u	student, truth, junior, revolution music,‡ usually,‡ future,‡ university‡
u . . . e	rule, June, include, introduce, blue, true use,‡ cute,‡ confuse,‡ argue‡

Other spellings:

o	do, to, who, movie
o . . . e	whose, lose, move, prove, shoe
ou	you, group, soup
ough	through
ew	new, grew, flew, threw, jewelry few,‡ view‡
ui	suit, fruit, juice
eau	beauty‡

*Some people pronounce these words with the sound ʊ.
‡These words have a y sound before the uw: yuw.

UNIT 14
Review

LISTENING PRACTICE 🔲

1: ʌ	*2: ɑ*	*3: ɔ*	*4: ow*	*5: ʊ*	*6: uw*
uh . . .	ah!	aw!	oh!	ugh!	ooh!
	Polly	Paul	pole	pull	pool
done	Don	Dawn	don't		dune
luck	lock	law	low	look	Luke
	folly	fall	foal	full	fool

When you hear one of the words above, give the number for its sound. 🔲

Example: full
    [sound] 5

PRONUNCIATION PRACTICE 🔲

The words on the left have the sound ə in these phrases. Listen and repeat:

at	looking at me
the	the pool
a	a pole
to	threw it to me
some	some clothes
of a	all of a sudden
you	What did you do?
and	Polly and Paul

DIALOGUE 🔲

Polly and Paul

Don: Ooh! Dawn! What happened to you? Did you fall into the pool?

Dawn: No. Polly and Paul pushed me. Ugh! That water is cold!

Don: Why did they push you?

Dawn: I don't know. We were just fooling around at the pool. And all of a sudden they pushed me.

Don: Oh! What did you do?

Dawn: Well, I felt awfully foolish because everyone was looking at me. And I . . . uh . . . couldn't swim because I had all my clothes on – my shoes, too.

Don: What did Polly and Paul do?
Dawn: Nothing! But Mr. Lucas was there and he was very good. He got a
        pole and threw it to me. Then he pulled me out of the pool.
Don: Huh. Polly and Paul. I'll have to talk to those two. They do some
        pretty stupid things sometimes.

PUZZLE

Which Word Doesn't Belong?   Which word does not have the same vowel sound
as the others?

Example:

>   but   sometimes   (put)   much   cousin

1. modern   got   popular   joking   clock

2. shoes   movie   look   soon   boot

3. nothing   just   does   money   closed

4. book   food   woman   push   good

5. home   don't   only   love   goes

6. cold   thought   fall   awful   lost

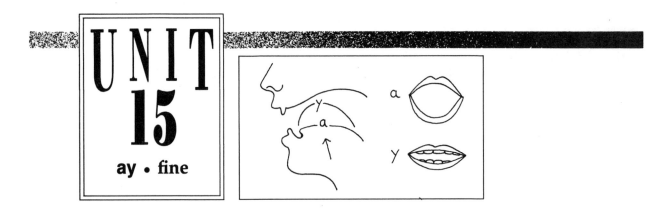

UNIT 15
ay • fine

This has two sounds: ɑ and y.
First practice the sound ɑ. This sound is long.
Now add y. This sound is short.

PRACTICE 1 📼

Listen and repeat:

	Sound 1	*Sound 2*	
	back	bike	
	hat	height	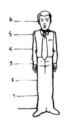
	van	vine	
	cat	kite	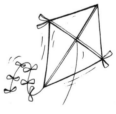
	pants	pints	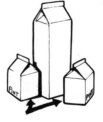

TEST 🔲

Look at these sentences. Circle the word in parentheses that you hear.

1. Carry it on your (back/bike).
2. There's a (van/vine) next to the house.
3. My (cat/kite) got stuck in a tree.
4. They (had/hide) the money.
5. Is this your (hat/height)?

PRACTICE 2 🔲

Listen and repeat:

Bye!	Myra	bike riding	typist
drive	Violet	ice skating	typewriter
mind	silence	spider	behind
like	smiling	library	ninety-nine
sometimes	climbing	tonight	

DIALOGUE 🔲

Mike, Myra, and Violet

(*Myra and Violet are typists at the library.*)

Myra: Hi, Mike!
Mike: Hello, Myra. Hello, Violet! You look really nice, Violet.
(*silence*)
Mike: I'm going out to buy ice cream. Would you like some, Violet?
Violet: No, thanks, Mike. I'm busy typing. Come back some other time. I have ninety-nine pages to type by Friday.
Mike: Oh, never mind your typing. Do you like ice skating, Violet?
Violet: Sometimes.
Mike: Would you like to go ice skating with me tonight?
Violet: Not tonight, Mike. I'm going for a drive with Simon.
Mike: How about Friday?
Violet: I'm going bike riding with Brian.
Mike: Hm! Oh, all right. Bye!
Myra: Violet, he put something behind your typewriter.
Violet: Something nice?
Myra: No. A spider.

CONVERSATION

Practice the words below. Then use them with a partner in the dialogue below.

flying	**ice** skating
climbing	**bike** riding
driving	**horse**back riding
hiking	

A: Do you like . . . ?
B: Yes. I like . . . a lot.   *or*   Sometimes.
A: Would you like to go . . . on Friday?
B: I can't on Friday. Maybe some other time.

ADDING -ing

Say these words and look at their spellings.

ride   fly   lie   fight   swim   fish

Which words have the sound **ay** (as in *fine*)?
Which words have the sound **ɪ** (as in *ship*)?

Now look at the *-ing* forms:

riding   flying   lying   fighting   swimming   fishing

Fill in the blank spaces with the base form of the verb or the *-ing* form:

Base Verb	*-ing*
ride	riding
drive	_____
sit	_____
_____	hiking
_____	typing
_____	smiling
_____	winning
cry	_____
light	_____
begin	_____
die	_____

SPELLING

The sound **ay** is usually written with the letters *i . . . e, i, igh,* or *y.*

i . . . e	time, nice, smile, crime, write, fine
i	hi, idea, Friday, exciting, final, bicycle, writing, library child, find, climb, pint, mind, ninth
igh	high, light, night, right, bright
y	cry, my, sky, fly, July, reply, psychologist
ie	die, pie, lie, tie
y . . . e	type, rhyme, style
ye	eye, dye, good-bye

Other spellings:

uy	buy, guy
ei	height
ai	aisle, Hawaii

UNIT 16

ɔy • boy

This has two sounds: ɔ and y.
First say ɔ.
Then add y. This part is short.

PRACTICE 1

Listen and repeat:

Sound 1	Sound 2
all	oil
ball	boil
jaw	Joy
raw	Roy
bald	boiled

TEST 🔲

Listen to these sentences. Circle the word in parentheses that you hear.

1. Is that (all/oil) in the salad?

2. Are they (bald/boiled)?

3. Is it (raw/Roy)?

4. The little boy was (bawling/boiling) with anger.

PRACTICE 2 🔲

Listen and repeat:

toy	Joyce	destroy
boys	enjoying	noisy
Roy	annoyed	spoiled
voices	annoying	

DIALOGUE 🔲

Noise

Roy: Boys! Stop making so much noise!
Boys: What?
Roy: Keep your voices down! YOU'RE MAKING TOO MUCH NOISE!
Joyce: Why are you so annoyed? They're enjoying themselves. They're little
        boys – of course they'll make noise.
Roy: Well, it's very annoying.
        (*raising his voice*) Boys!
Boys: (*continue making noise*)
Roy: They don't listen. They're spoiled. They destroy all the toys I buy
        them. And they're the noisiest boys I've ever heard. I'm sure I wasn't
        that noisy when I was a little boy.
Joyce: Well, maybe you shouldn't buy them such noisy toys.
Roy: It's not the toys that are noisy – it's the boys!

STRESS 🔲

Listen and repeat:

Kids make noise.
The **kids make noise.**
The **kids** will **make noise.**
The **kids** are **mak**ing **noise.**
The **kids** have been **mak**ing **noise.**

The last sentence is much longer than the first, but try to say all the sentences in about the same amount of time. Make sure you put stress only on the words in blacker type.

Now try this:

> **Buy new toys.**
> **Buy** them **new toys.**
> **Buy** them some **new toys.**
> You should **buy** them some **new toys.**

SPELLING

The sound ɔy is written with the letters *oi* or *oy*.

    oi   oil, boil, join, point, coin, spoil
            voice, choice, noise
    oy toy, boy, enjoy, destroy, annoy, loyal, employer

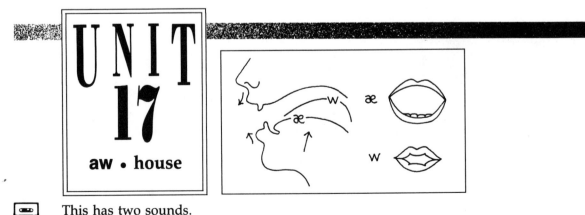

UNIT 17
aw • house

This has two sounds.
First practice the sound æ.
Now add w. This sound is short.

PRACTICE 1

Listen and repeat:

	Sound 1	*Sound 2*	
	shot	shout	
	Don	down	
R	R	hour	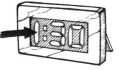
	pond	pound	
	Scot	scout	

TEST

Listen to these sentences. Circle the word in parentheses that you hear.

1. We saw a group of (Scots/scouts).
2. Is it one (R/hour) or two?
3. Are you going (, Don/down)?
4. The (shots/shouts) woke me.
5. How many (ponds/pounds) are there?

PRACTICE 2

Listen and repeat:

Ow!	found	loudly	house
how	around	shouting	couch
now	upside down	out	town
brown	somehow	mouse	

DIALOGUE

A Mouse in the House

Mrs. Brown:	(*shouting loudly*) I'VE FOUND A MOUSE!
Mr. Brown:	Ow! Don't shout so loud. Calm down! Please stop shouting and sit down.
Mrs. Brown:	(*sitting down*) I found a mouse in the house.
Mr. Brown:	A brown mouse?
Mrs. Brown:	Yes. A little brown mouse. It was running around in the living room.
Mr. Brown:	Where is it now?
Mrs. Brown:	It's under the couch now.
Mr. Brown:	Well, get it out.
Mrs. Brown:	How?
Mr. Brown:	Move the couch around. Turn it upside down. You can get it out somehow. We don't want a mouse in our house. We have the cleanest house in town!

STRESS

Example 1:

Sit down.

Listen and repeat:

He's **sitting down**.
He's **standing up**.
He's **lying down**.
He's **turning around**.
He's **going out**.
He's **running around**.

Match these pictures with the correct sentences.

a)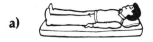

b)

c)

d)

e)

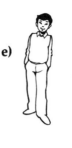

f)

Example 2:

>**Get** it **out**.

Listen and repeat:

>**Put** it **down**.
>**Throw** it **out**.
>**Turn** it **down**.
>**Fill** it **out**.
>**Cross** it **out**.
>**Take** it **out**.

Match these pictures with the correct sentences.

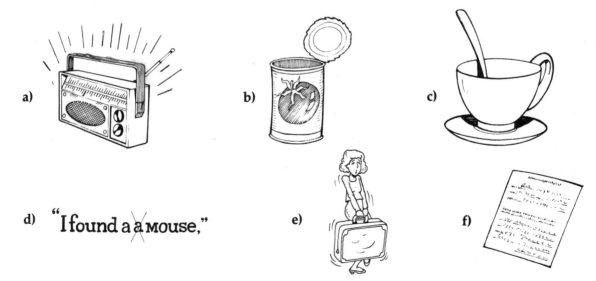

a)

b)

c)

d) "I found a a̶ mouse,"

e)

f)

SPELLING

The sound **aw** is written with the letters *ou* or *ow*.

>*ou*   about, around, found, sound, mouth, south, without, thousand
>house, mouse, pronounce
>*ow*   down, crowd, town, brown, now, how, allow, vowel

UNIT 18
Review

LISTENING PRACTICE

<u>1: ay</u>	<u>2: ɔy</u>	<u>3: aw</u>
buy	boy	bow
aisle	oil	owl
tile	toil	towel
lied	Lloyd	loud

When you hear one of the words above, give the number for its sound.

Example: boy
[sound] 2

DIALOGUE

A Boy Lying Down

Joy: Do you like this painting?
Roy: Is that a boy?
Joy: Yes. I'm trying to paint a boy lying on the ground.
Roy: Hm. . . . Why don't you buy some oil paints?
Joy: I don't enjoy painting with oils.
Roy: It's nice, but why is there a big brown cloud behind the boy?
Joy: (*pointing*) It's not a cloud. It's a mountain.

List three (or more) words from the dialogue that have the sounds below.

	1 ay	2 ɔy	3 aw
1.	*like*	*boy*	*down*
2.			
3.			
4.			

UNIT 19

ə • Review
a camera

PRACTICE 1 🔲

Word Stress   In English words with more than one syllable, one syllable has a strong stress. The other syllables have a weaker stress or no stress. Unstressed syllables very often have the sound ə. In the words below, there is a dot under the vowel letters pronounced as ə.

Some English words have strong stress on the last syllable. Listen and repeat:

again	decide	repeat
asleep	forget	pronounce
below	o'clock	afternoon
began	herself	understand

Some words have strong stress in the middle. Listen and repeat:

Anita	tomorrow
America	conversation
binoculars	

But most words have strong stress on the first syllable. Listen and repeat:

sister	quarter	breakfast	quietly
brother	closet	camera	photograph
water	seven	wonderful	Saturday
better	listen	beautiful	
answer	opened	comfortable	

PRACTICE 2 🔲

Sentence Stress   In the words on the right, the spelling has been changed to show you when to use the sound ə. Listen and repeat:

a photograph of Anita   1   ə photəgraph əf ənitə

a glass of water   2   ə glass əf watər

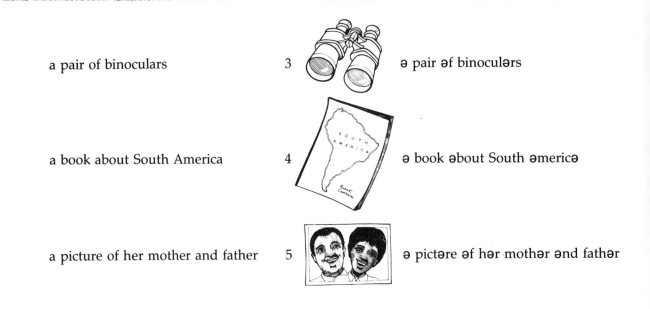

a pair of binoculars   3   ə pair əf binoculərs

a book about South America   4   ə book əbout South əmericə

a picture of her mother and father   5   ə pictəre əf hər mothər ənd fathər

Now cover the words on the left and practice questions and answers about the pictures.
Example:

> What's in picture 2?
> ə glass əf watər

Listen and repeat:

She's looking at the clock.   1   She's looking ət thə clock.

She's closing her eyes.   2   She's closing hər eyes.

They're having some breakfast.   3   They're having səme breakfəst.

I'd love to go to South America.   4   I'd love tə go tə South əmericə.

Now cover the words on the left and practice questions and answers.

Example:

> What's she doing in picture 1?
> She's looking ət thə clock.

PRACTICE 3

Listen and repeat:

Do you have the time?	Də yə have thə time?
It's six o'clock.	It's six ə'clock.
It's a quarter to seven.	It's ə quartər tə sevən.

Now practice these:

Example:

> A: Do you have the time?
> B: Yes. It's a quarter to twelve.

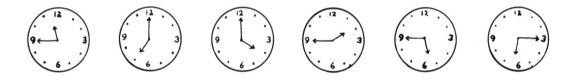

READING 💬

Listen to the story. Then practice reading it aloud. There is a dot under the vowels pronounced as ə.

Ạnitạ spent Satụrday afternoon looking ạt ạ beautịfụl book ạbout South Ạmericạ.

"I'd love tọ go tọ South Ạmericạ," she said tọ hẹrself.

The next morning, when Ạnitạ woke up it wạs six ọ'clock, ạnd her brothẹrs ạnd sisters wẹre still ạsleep. Ạnitạ looked ạt thẹm ạnd closed her eyes ạgain.

Then she quietly got out ọf bed ạnd began tọ pack ạ suitcase. She took sọme comfortạble clothes out ọf thẹ closet. She packed ạ pair ọf binocụlạrs ạnd her sistẹr's camerạ. She also decided tọ pack ạ photọgraph ọf hẹrself ạnd one ọf her mothẹr ạnd fathẹr.

"I'd bettẹr not forget tọ have sọme breakfạst," she said tọ hẹrself. But then she looked ạt thẹ clock. It wạs ạ quartẹr tọ sevẹn.

"I'm going tọ* be late," she said. "I'll just drink ạ glass ọf watẹr."

"Ạ glass ọf watẹr," she said.

"Watẹr," she said, ạnd opẹned her eyes.

She wạs still in bed, ạnd her brothẹrs ạnd sisters wẹre laughing ạt her.

"Tell ụs what yọu wẹre dreaming ạbout," they said tọ her.

But Ạnitạ didn't answẹr. She wạs thinking ạbout her wondẹrful trip tọ South Ạmericạ.

*Going to (to indicate future) is often pronounced **gʌnə**.

U N I T 20

3r • word

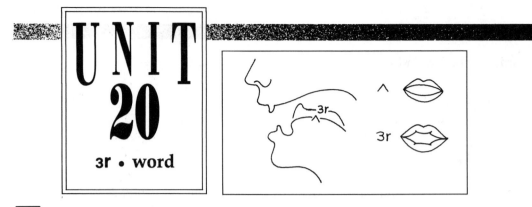

First practice the sound ʌ.
Now curl the tip of your tongue up and back a little.
3r is pronounced together as one sound. It is the same as ər, but stressed.

PRACTICE 1

Listen and repeat:

	Sound 1	*Sound 2*	
	torn	turn	
	shorts	shirts	
	four	fur	
	ward	word	**Two Words**
	walk	work	

PRACTICE 2

Listen and repeat:

	Sound 1	*Sound 2*	
	far	fur	
	star	stir	
	barn	burn	
	hearts	hurts	
	hard	heard	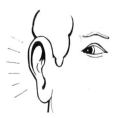

PRACTICE 3

Listen and repeat:

	Sound 1	*Sound 2*	
	shut	shirt	
	huts	hurts	
	bun	burn	
	bud	bird	
	gull	girl	

TEST ▭

Listen to these sentences. Circle the word in parentheses that you hear.

1. Is it (four/far/fur)?
2. It was spring, and the tree was covered with (buds/birds).
3. That's a very big (ward/word).
4. Can you (walk/work) faster?
5. Those (barns/buns/burns) don't look good to me.
6. Look at all the (gulls/girls) on the beach.

PRACTICE 4 ▭

Listen and repeat:

nurse	skirts	Herb Turner	Pearl
work	early	colonel	thirsty
hurts	world	were	dirty
curse	Thursday	weren't	worst
shirts	Sherman	Gertrude	

DIALOGUE ▭

The Worst Nurse

Herb Turner:	Nurse!
Colonel Sherman:	Nurse! I'm thirsty!
Herb Turner:	Nurse! My head hurts!
Colonel Sherman:	NURSE!
Herb Turner:	Curse these nurses!
Colonel Sherman:	That nurse Gertrude always wears such dirty shirts.
Herb Turner:	And such short skirts.
Colonel Sherman:	She always leaves work early.
Herb Turner:	She and . . . er . . . that other nurse, Pearl, weren't at work on Thursday, were they?
Colonel Sherman:	No, they weren't.
Herb Turner:	Gertrude is the worst nurse in the ward, isn't she?
Colonel Sherman:	No – she's the worst nurse in the world!

INTONATION ▭

Tag Questions   Tag questions have a falling tone when a person is making a comment or giving an opinion and expects the other person to agree.

Listen and repeat:

were they?   **were** we?   **were** you?

They weren't at **work**,   **were** they?

We weren't **early**,   **were** we?

Practice in pairs:

Example 1:   We weren't early.

   A: We weren't **early**, **were** we?

   B: No, we **were**n't.

Example 2:   You weren't early.

   A: You weren't **early**, **were** you?

   B: No, I **was**n't.

1. We weren't the worst.

2. You weren't first.

3. Those girls weren't German.

4. You weren't at work.

5. Those skirts weren't hers.

6. We weren't learning any new words.

7. The nurses weren't walking to work.

8. You weren't thirsty.

SPELLING

The sound 3r is spelled many different ways.

er	her, person, weren't, certain, term, service, verb, perfect, prefer, preferred
ir	bird, first, girl, shirt, skirt, thirsty, thirty, thirteen, dirty, stir
ur	Thursday, nurse, fur, curtain, hurt, turn, burn, purpose, occur
or	word, work, world, worse, worst, worry*

Other spellings:

ear	early, earth, earn, learn, heard, search
our	courage,* journey

*Some people say these words with the vowel ʌ instead of 3.

Section B

Consonants

VOCABULARY

First learn the words you will need in order to study how to make the sounds in this section.

YOUR MOUTH

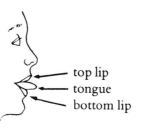
top lip
tongue
bottom lip

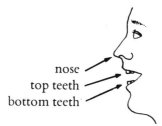
nose
top teeth
bottom teeth

Practice:

1. Touch your
   | top lip
   | top teeth
   | bottom lip | with your finger.
   | bottom teeth
   | tongue
   | nose

2. Open your lips.   Close your lips.   Close your lips tight.   Make your lips round.

INSIDE YOUR MOUTH

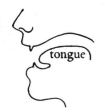
tongue

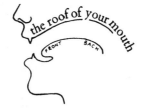
the roof of your mouth
FRONT   BACK

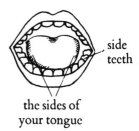
side teeth
the sides of your tongue

Practice:

1. Touch
   | your top teeth
   | your bottom teeth | with your tongue.
   | the roof of your mouth

2. Touch your side teeth with the sides of your tongue.

3. Touch the front of the roof of your mouth with the front of your tongue.

Touch the back of the roof of your mouth with the back of your tongue.

AIR

1. Hold a piece of paper in front of your mouth.

When you blow out air the paper moves.

Air is coming through your mouth.

2. Close your mouth.

Push air forward in your mouth.

VOICE

Put your hand on the front of your neck.

When you sing, you can feel your voice. You are using your voice.

The sound of your voice is coming through your mouth.

UNIT 21

p • pen

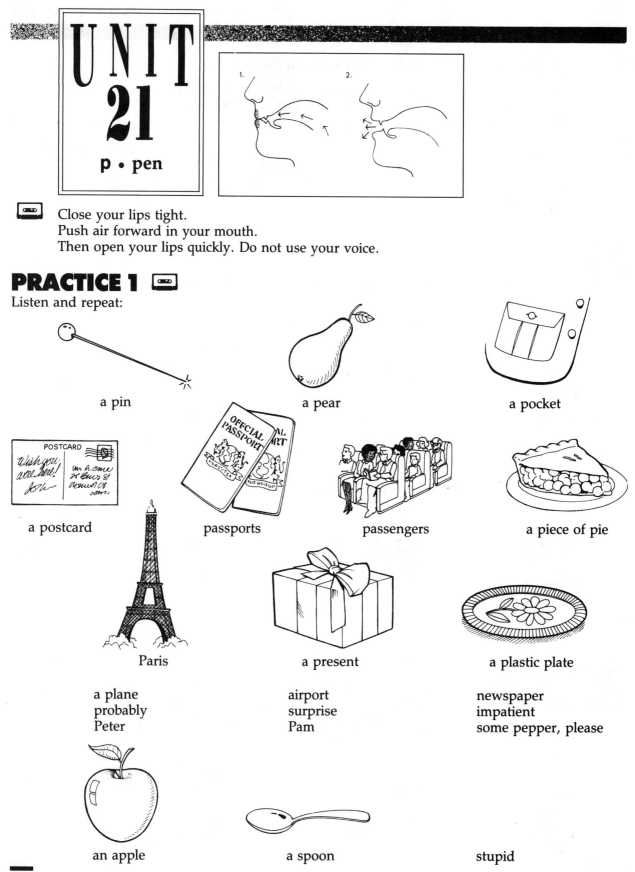

Close your lips tight.
Push air forward in your mouth.
Then open your lips quickly. Do not use your voice.

PRACTICE 1

Listen and repeat:

a pin

a pear

a pocket

a postcard

passports

passengers

a piece of pie

Paris

a present

a plastic plate

a plane
probably
Peter

airport
surprise
Pam

newspaper
impatient
some pepper, please

an apple

a spoon

stupid

PRACTICE 2 🔊

Listen and repeat. The sound **p** is quieter in these words:

a stamp

an envelope

Help!

a cup	help me
helpful	Chapman
upstairs	stop pulling
dropped	stop shouting
perhaps	stop talking
empty	

DIALOGUE 🔊

Passports, Please

(Mr. and Mrs. Chapman are at the airport. They have just gotten off the plane from Paris.)

Official:	Passports, please.
Mr. Chapman:	I think I've lost our passports, Pam.
Mrs. Chapman:	Oh, Peter, how could you be so stupid? Didn't you put them in your pocket?
Mr. Chapman:	*(emptying his pockets)* Here's a pen . . . a pencil . . . a postcard . . . an envelope . . . a stamp . . . a pin . . .
Mrs. Chapman:	Oh, stop taking everything out of your pockets. You probably put them in the plastic bag.
Mr. Chapman:	*(emptying the plastic bag)* Here's a newspaper . . . an apple . . . a pear . . . a plastic cup . . . a spoon . . . some paper plates . . . a piece of pie . . . some pepper . . . some presents . . .
Mrs. Chapman:	Oh, stop pulling everything out of the plastic bag, Peter. These people are getting impatient.
Mr. Chapman:	Well, help me, Pam.
Mrs. Chapman:	We've lost our passports. Perhaps we dropped them on the plane.
Official:	Then let the other passengers past, please.
Mr. Chapman:	Pam, why don't you help? You're not being very helpful. Put the things in the plastic bag.
Official:	Your name, please?
Mr. Chapman:	Chapman.
Official:	Please go upstairs with this police officer, Mr. Chapman.

INTONATION 🔲

Making a List   In making a list, there is usually a rising tone on all the items before the last. There is a falling tone on the last item.

Listen and repeat:

I'm bringing **ap**ples.

I'm bringing **ap**ples and **Peter's** bringing **pears**.

I'm bringing **ap**ples, **Peter's** bringing **pears**, and **Pam's** bringing pota**to** chips.

GAME

"We're Having a Picnic"

Example:

A: We're having a picnic and I'm bringing pears.

B: We're having a picnic. A is bringing pears and I'm bringing potato chips.

C: We're having a picnic. A is bringing pears, B is bringing potato chips, and I'm bringing soup.

Each student adds something to the list. You must remember what the other students have said.

Practice the words in the list before you start. Try to add other words of your own with the sound p in them.

apples	**nap**kins	**soup**
pears	**paper plates**	**shrimp**
peanuts	**plas**tic **cups**	**spin**ach
pota**to** chips	**spoons**	spa**ghet**ti
a **pine**apple	**pizza**	a **pic**nic basket
pie	**pep**per	a **plas**tic **spi**der

SPELLING

The sound p is written with the letter *p*:

p   paper, people, passport, plastic, probably, surprise, supermarket, envelope, stamp

pp   pepper, happy, supper

shop – shopping, stop – stopped, slip – slipped, drop – dropped

The letter *p* is silent in these words:

psychology, psychiatrist, pneumonia, corps, raspberry, receipt, cupboard

UNIT 22

b • baby

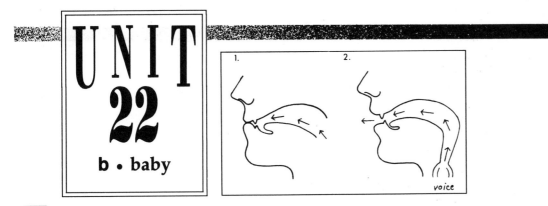

First practice p.
Use your voice to make b.

PRACTICE 1

Listen and repeat:

	Sound 1	*Sound 2*	
	pie	buy	
	pear	bear	
	path	bath	
	cap	cab	
	rope	robe	

TEST ▱

Listen to these sentences. Circle the word in parentheses that you hear.

1. There are (pears/bears) in the garden.
2. Could you tell me where the (path/bath) is?
3. She threw away her old (pills/bills).
4. I took a yellow (cap/cab).
5. Put the (rope/robe) in the closet.

PRACTICE 2 ▱

Listen and repeat:

busy	blouse	remember	February
built	blue	somebody	cab
birds	bracelet	Robin	job
about	brother	terrible	club
beautiful	Barbara's birthday	celebrate	Bob

DIALOGUE ▱

Barbara's Birthday

Barbara: Hi, Bob!
Bob: Hi, Barbara. You seem very happy.
Barbara: (*pause*) Well. . . . You know, today's my birthday.
Bob: Oh, right. February 7th. Your birthday! Happy birthday, Barbara!
Barbara: Thanks, Bob. Look at this bracelet that Robin gave me. Isn't it beautiful?
Bob: Oh, it is. That's a beautiful blouse, too. You look good in blue. Was that a birthday present, too?
Barbara: Yes. And my mother gave me some paintbrushes and a book about birds. And, uh, somebody bought me a cookbook.
Bob: Did your brother give you anything?
Barbara: Yes. He built some bookshelves for my bedroom.
Bob: I'm really sorry, Barbara, but I forgot all about your birthday. I've been so busy with my job. And I'm terrible at remembering birthdays, anyway.
Barbara: Well, my birthday isn't over yet . . .
Bob: Yeah! Let's go out and celebrate. We can get a cab and go to that new club.

STRESS ▱

Noun Compounds   Listen and repeat:

1. a **shelf**   a **book**shelf
2. a **brush**   a **hair**brush
             a **paint**brush
3. a **card**   a **post**card   a **birth**day card
4. a **ball**   a **bas**ketball   a **ping**-pong ball
5. a **bag**   a **hand**bag   a **shop**ping bag
6. a **book**   a **cook**book   a bi**ol**ogy book

CONVERSATION

Do this in pairs. Talk about these pictures. Follow the example.

Example:

    A: I hear you gave Barbara a shelf for her birthday.

    B: Yes, I gave her a bookshelf.

1. bag

2. ball

3. ball

4. bag

5. brush

6. card

7. book

8. book

9. brush

10. card

SPELLING

The sound **b** is written with the letter *b*:

    b   baby, about, birthday, brother, library, terrible, problem, job

    bb rubber, bubble

          rob – robber

The letter *b* is silent in:

    climb, lamb, thumb, comb, bom<u>b</u>

    doubt, debt, subtle

UNIT 23

t • tie

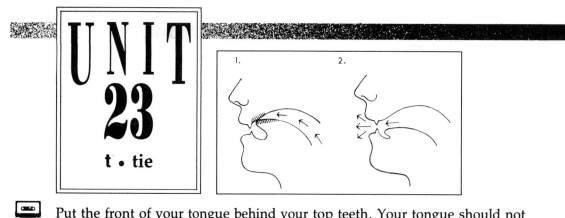

Put the front of your tongue behind your top teeth. Your tongue should not touch your teeth. Push air forward in your mouth.
Then move your tongue away. Do not use your voice.

PRACTICE 1

Listen and repeat:

tie

top

cafeteria

thirteen
fourteen

tell the time
ten to ten

toy

tape recorder

teenager

towels

twins

twelve
twenty

telephone

return

try

PRACTICE 2

Listen and repeat. *t* is very quiet in these words:

hat

racket

football

jacket	next
shirt	basement
left	department
first	a hot meal

PRACTICE 3

Listen and repeat:

stereo

upstairs

shirts

skirts

students	it's
straight	restaurant
hats	sportswear

PRACTICE 4

Listen and repeat. *t* sounds like a quick d in these words:

sweater

letter

elevator

typewriter

city	little
water	sporting goods

```
┌─────────────────────────────────────────────────────────────────┐
│  CITY TOWER DEPARTMENT STORE — THE WORLD'S TALLEST STORE          │
│                      Store Directory                              │
│                                                                   │
│   Basement                        Third Floor                     │
│   Sheets and towels               Toy Department                  │
│   Restaurant                                                      │
│                                   Tenth Floor                      │
│   First Floor (street level)      Televisions, stereos, typewriters│
│   Women's coats and jackets                                       │
│   Hats                            Twelfth Floor                    │
│   Belts                           Sporting goods department        │
│                                   (tennis rackets, baseball bats, etc.)│
│   Second Floor                                                    │
│   Men's clothing (suits, ties, shirts,   Telephone               │
│   pants, sweaters, coats, jackets)                               │
│                                   Thirteenth Floor                 │
│   Women's sportswear (skirts,     Cafeteria                       │
│   pants, sweaters)                Returns department              │
└─────────────────────────────────────────────────────────────────┘
```

DIALOGUE ⌷▭⌷

In a Department Store

Teenage girl:	I want to* buy a | hat. | jacket.
Salesperson:	Hats | are downstairs on the first floor. Jackets |
Tall woman:	I'd like to buy a skirt.
Salesperson:	Skirts are in the sportswear department, to your left.
Student:	Where can I get a | typewriter? | tape recorder? | stereo?
Salesperson:	Take the elevator to the tenth floor.
Short man:	Where would I find | ties? | shirts?
Salesperson:	The men's department is straight ahead.
Fat man:	Where can I get a hot meal?
Salesperson:	There's a | cafeteria on the thirteenth floor. | restaurant in the basement.
Little girl:	Could you tell me where the toy department is?
Salesperson:	Certainly. It's upstairs on the next floor.
Tall man:	I want to return this sweater. It's too tight.
Salesperson:	The returns department is on the top floor, next to the cafeteria.
Short woman:	I want to buy some | towels. | sheets.
Salesperson:	Take the stairs down to the basement.
Teenage boy:	Where can I get a | tennis racket? | baseball bat? | football?
Salesperson:	Try the sporting goods department, on the twelfth floor.
Twins:	Could you tell us the time, please?
Salesperson:	Yes. It's exactly twenty-two minutes after ten.

*want to is often pronounced as wanə.

CONVERSATION

Read the dialogue again and then practice in pairs:

Examples:

A: Could you tell me where the cafeteria is?
B: Yes. It's on the thirteenth floor.

A: Where can I get a coat?
B: The coat department is on the first floor.

One person should ask for things like these:

cafe**teri**a	**tie**
telephone	**hat**
sportswear department	**sweat**er

The other person should answer, using the store directory. Use words like these:

tenth	**next**
first	down**stairs**
basement	to the **left**
top	**straight** a**head**

SPELLING

The sound t is spelled with the letter *t*:

t   time, try, twelve, straight, restaurant, department, sweater, city, write, minute, late

tt   letter, matter, little, bottle, attempt, attend
       sit – sitting, get – getting, hot – hotter, wet – wetter

Other spellings:

th   Thomas

The letter *t* is silent in:

listen, whistle, castle, Christmas, often, mus<u>t</u>n't, ballet, mortgage

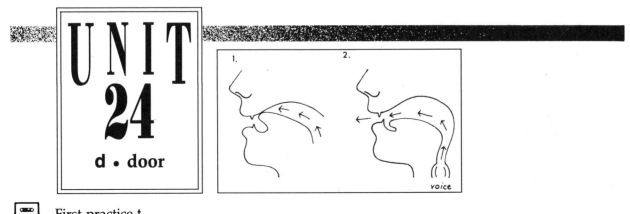

UNIT
24
d • door

1.   2.

voice

First practice t.
Use your voice to make d.

PRACTICE 1

Listen and repeat:

Sound 1   Sound 2

 tore   door

 time   dime

 train   drain

 write   ride

 cart   card

TEST

Listen to these sentences. Circle the word in parentheses that you hear.

1. I want to (try/dry) this shirt.
2. Do you have the (time/dime)?
3. That's a good (cart/card).
4. She (writes/rides) very well.
5. We (sent/send) all the packages airmail.

PRACTICE 2 🔲
Listen and repeat:

date	tried	decided	Judy
Debbie	stayed	told	records
dancing	rained	hard	children
yesterday	happened	Donald	a bad cold
today	answered	David	didn't
nobody	damaged	did	

DIALOGUE 🔲
A Missed Date

Debbie: Hello.

Donald: Hello, Debbie? This is Donald.

Debbie: Oh, hi, Donald.

Donald: What happened yesterday? You forgot our date, didn't you?

Debbie: Well, it rained hard all day and I had a bad cold, so I decided to stay home.

Donald: You did? But I tried to call you at least twenty times and nobody answered.

Debbie: Oh, the telephone lines were damaged by the storm. They repaired them today.

Donald: What did David do yesterday? Did he and Judy go dancing?

Debbie: No. They stayed home and played cards with the children.

Donald: And what did you do? Did you play cards, too?

Debbie: No. I listened to records and studied. What did you do yesterday, Donald?

Donald: I just told you, Debbie. I tried to call you twenty times!

PRONUNCIATION 🔲

-ed **endings**   Listen and repeat:

-ed = d	*-ed* = t	*-ed* = ɪd
rain*ed*	laugh*ed*	wait*ed*
play*ed*	brush*ed*	decid*ed*
fill*ed*	watch*ed*	paint*ed*
clos*ed*	danc*ed*	shout*ed*

How many syllables are there in   rain?
rained?
laugh?
laughed?
wait?
waited?
need?
needed?

CONVERSATION

Talk about these pictures.

Example:

studied all night
listened to the radio

A: He studied all night, didn't he?
B: No, he didn't. He listened to the radio.

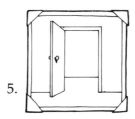

1. combed his hair
brushed it

2. cried a lot
laughed a lot

3. painted the room
cleaned it

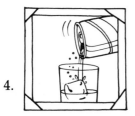

4. emptied the glass
filled it

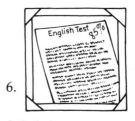

5. closed the door
opened it

6. failed the test
passed it

7. walked to work
waited for the bus

8. pulled the car
pushed it

SPELLING

The sound d is written with the letter *d:*

  d   door, date, didn't, nobody, ready, study, studied, hard, cold, understand,
       decide

  dd address, sudden, ladder, middle, add
       sad – sadder, mud – muddy

The letter *d* is silent in:
       handkerchief, handsome, We<u>d</u>nesday

UNIT 25

k • key

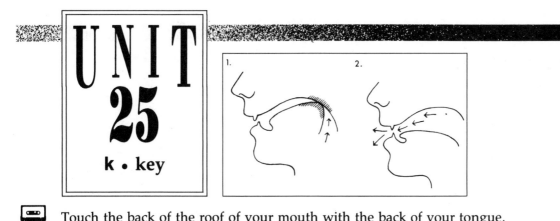

Touch the back of the roof of your mouth with the back of your tongue.
Push air forward in your mouth.
Then move your tongue away. Do not use your voice.

PRACTICE 1

Listen and repeat:

car

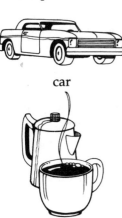

key

cuckoo

cup of coffee

clock

chocolate cookies

bookcase
Canada
Christine
question

cream
comfortable
Claudia
quiet

crowded
of course
cute
quite

sky

ski

excuse me

PRACTICE 2

Listen and repeat. k is usually quieter here:

look	electric	thanks
bake	thank you	next
like	take two	looked
oak	expensive	talked
milk	expired	exactly
plastic	six	

DIALOGUE

The Cuckoo Clock

Christine: Would you like cream in your coffee, Claudia?
Claudia: No, thank you. But I'd like some milk, please.
Christine: Would you like some chocolate cookies?
Claudia: Mm, yes. Thanks. Did you bake these?
Christine: Yes. Take some more. And here's . . .
Claudia: Excuse me, Christine. But what's that next to your bookcase? Is it a clock?
Christine: Yes. It's a cuckoo clock. I got it in Canada.
Claudia: Is it plastic?
Christine: Oh, no. It's oak. It was quite an expensive clock. It's electric.
Claudia: Well, it's exactly six o'clock now, and it's very quiet. Doesn't it say cuckoo?
Christine: Of course, Claudia. Look!
Clock: Cuckoo! Cuckoo! Cuckoo! Cuckoo! Cuckoo! Cuckoo!
Claudia: Oh! What a cute clock!
Clock: Cuckoo!

STRESS

Listen and repeat:

a **black cup**	a **black cof**fee **cup**
an **emp**ty **bot**tle	an **emp**ty **Coke** bottle
a **com**fortable **jacket**	a **com**fortable **ski** jacket
an e**lec**tric **clock**	an e**lec**tric **cuck**oo clock
a **clean knife**	a **clean steak** knife

JUMBLED SENTENCES

Do this in pairs.

Example: cup a **cof**fee black it's
    A: What's that?
    B: It's a black coffee cup.

1.   an it's **cuck**oo electric clock

2.   ring plastic it's **key** a

3.   crowded it's car a **sub**way

4.   it's bottle empty an **Coke**

5.   book ad**dress** a it's black

6.   chocolate cone cream **ice** a it's

7.   it's **ski** comfortable jacket a

8.   card an **cred**it it's expired

9.   **truck** angry it's driver an

SPELLING

The sound **k** is usually written with the letters *k, c,* or *ck.*

  k   key, kind, ask, think, sky, talk, market, like, bake, take
  c   car, could, crowded, doctor, chocolate, electric, cute
  cc occur, accountant, occasion
  cc (pronounced **ks** before the letters *e* or *i*) accept, success, accent, accident
  ck back, sick; clock, jacket

Other spellings:

  ch school, chemistry, mechanic, echo, architect, stomach, headache
  x   (pronounced **ks**) six, next, box, taxi, extra, expensive
  xc except, exciting, excellent
  qu (pronounced **kw**) quiet, quite, quick, question, square
  qu (pronounced **k**) mosquito, conquer, technique, mosque

The letter *k* is silent before *n* at the beginning of a word:

    know, knife, knee

UNIT 26

g · girl

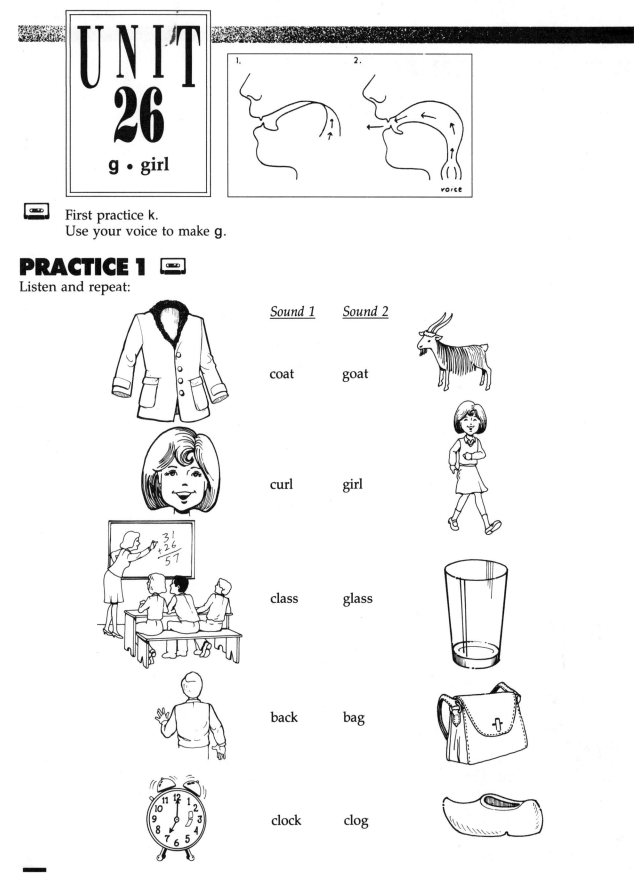

First practice k.
Use your voice to make **g**.

PRACTICE 1

Listen and repeat:

Sound 1	Sound 2
coat	goat
curl	girl
class	glass
back	bag
clock	clog

TEST 🔲

Listen to these sentences. Circle the word in parentheses that you hear.

1. Have you seen his new (coat/goat)?
2. There's a spider on your (back/bag).
3. How many (classes/glasses) do you have?
4. That store sells (clocks/clogs).
5. What a cute little (curl/girl)!

PRACTICE 2 🔲

Listen and repeat:

get	August	Margaret	grass
good	beginning	Greek	great
guitar	together	Greg	glad
guests	again	Craig	dog
golf	Chicago	telegram	England
garden	jogging		

DIALOGUE 🔲

Guests in August

Craig: I just got a telegram from Margaret and Greg.
Gloria: Are they coming to Chicago again?
Craig: Yes. They're coming the beginning of August.
Gloria: Oh, good! We can all get together again.
Craig: I'm glad they're coming in August. Maybe Greg and I can play some golf or get tickets to a baseball game.
Gloria: And Margaret and I can take the dog and go jogging in the park.
Craig: Remember the garden party they gave when we were in England?
Gloria: Oh, yes. We all sat on the grass, and Margaret played her guitar and sang Greek songs.
Craig: I had a great time. It'll be good to see them again.

STRESS 🔲

Here is the telegram
from Margaret and Greg:

> ARRIVING CHICAGO
>
> BEGINNING AUGUST

This is what it means:

We're arriving in Chicago at the beginning of August.

This is much longer, but try to say both sentences in the same length of time. Listen and repeat:

ar**ri**ving Chi**ca**go be**gin**ning **Au**gust
We're ar**ri**ving in Chi**ca**go at the be**gin**ning of **Au**gust.

Now try these:

1. **Glad coming August.**
   We're **glad** you're **com**ing in **Aug**ust.

2. **Bring dog, golf** clubs.
   Bring your **dog** and your **golf** clubs.

3. **Bring** guitar.
   Bring your gui**tar**.

4. **Lost** guitar. **Pos**sible **send cash**?
   I **lost** my guitar. Would it be **pos**sible to **send** me some **cash**?

5. For**get** guitar. **Bring dog**.
   For**get** about your gui**tar**, but **bring** your **dog**.

SPELLING

The sound **g** is usually written with the letter *g* or the letters *gu*.

- *g*   garden, again, telegram, August, grass, forget, begin, dog
- *gg* egg
       beg – beggar, jog – jogging, fog – foggy
- *gu* guest, guitar, guard, guess, guide, dialogue

Other spellings:

- *gh* ghost, spaghetti, Pittsburgh
- *x*   (pronounced **gz**) example, exist, exactly, exam

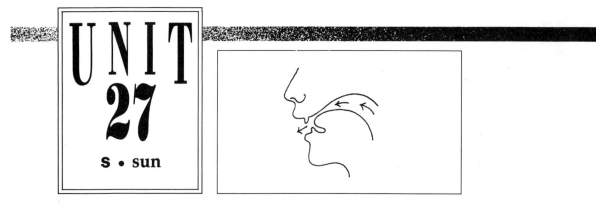

Touch your side teeth with the sides of your tongue.
Put your tongue forward.
Force air out over the top of your tongue, making a hissing sound.
Do not use your voice.

PRACTICE 1 📼

Listen and repeat:

Sue

sea

sip

bus

piece

price

PRACTICE 2 📼

Listen and repeat:

sit	seashore	it's	spend
Sam	sensible	let's	sleep
sand	outside	that's	swimming
Saturday	Alice	six	waterskiing
Sunday	instead	star	expensive
sailing	just	stay	exciting

DIALOGUE 📼

It's Expensive

Sam: Let's go to the seashore on Saturday.

Alice: Yes! Let's go sailing and waterskiing. That's so exciting.

Sam: It's expensive, too. Let's just sit in the sun and go swimming instead.

Alice: Let's stay over Saturday night and spend Sunday there, too. We could stay at the Six Star Hotel.

Sam: Be sensible, Alice. It's too expensive. Let's sleep outside instead.

Alice: Yes. Let's sleep on the sand. That's more exciting.

JOINING SOUNDS

Listen and repeat:

Let's sit in the sun.

Let's stay in a hotel.

Let's sleep outside.

Let's spend Sunday there, too.

Let's just sit on the sand.

He smokes cigarettes.

She likes sports.

He speaks slowly.

DRILL

Example:

A: I like cats.

B: Sam likes cats, too.

1. I hate hats.

2. I smoke cigarettes.

3. I eat lots of carrots.

4. I laugh at silly jokes.

5. I want some books.

6. I take photographs.

7. I collect stamps.

8. I get headaches.

CONVERSATION

Practice in pairs.

Example:

A: Should we go to the **sea**shore or stay **home**?

B: Let's | go to the **sea**shore.
        | stay **home**.

1. Should we take a basket or a suitcase?

2. Should we go sailing or waterskiing?

3. Should we go swimming or just sit in the sun?

4. Should we eat ice cream or potato chips?

5. Should we sit on a seat or on the sand?

6. Should we stay in an expensive hotel or sleep outside?

7. Should we be sensible or silly?

READING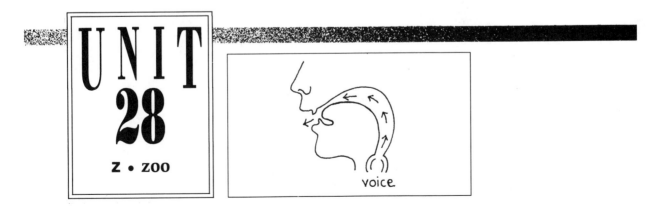

Listen:

The Smile of a Snake

She speaks slowly and smokes special, expensive cigarettes. As she steps upstairs, her long skirt sweeps over her silver slippers. She is small and smart and sweet-looking. Her skin is like snow.

"You have stolen my heart!" I once said stupidly, and she smiled. But when she smiled, she smiled the smile of a snake.

Now practice reading this aloud.

SPELLING

The sound **s** is usually written with the letter *s*:

- *s*   sun, sister, stop, smile, special, just, sensible, opposite, person, stamps, curious, bus
- *ss*   class, lesson, address, across, grass, kiss, possible
- *se*   horse, house, worse, purpose, promise, false, sense, use (noun), close (adjective)

Other spellings:

- *c*   (before *e, i,* or *y*) cent, ceiling, city, pencil, exercise, bicycle
- *ce*   police, face, dance, nice, office, once, place, piece
- *sc*   scene, science, scent, muscle
- *x*   (pronounced **ks**) six, box, taxi, exercise, expensive, next
- *cc*   (pronounced **ks**) success, accent
- *ps*   psychology, psychiatrist
- *st*   listen, castle, Christmas
- *sw*   answer, sword

The letter *s* is silent in these words:

island, aisle, corps

First practice **s**.
Use your voice to make **z**.

PRACTICE 1 📼

Listen and repeat:

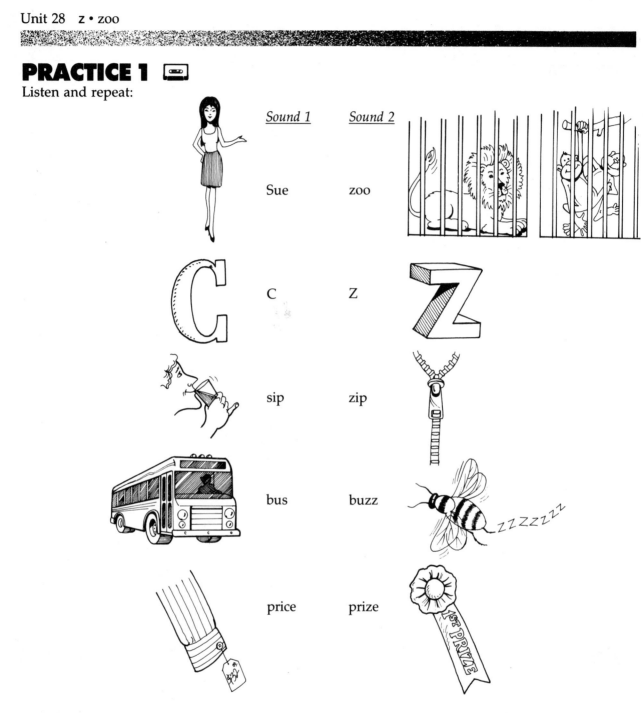

	Sound 1	Sound 2	
	Sue	zoo	
	C	Z	
	sip	zip	
	bus	buzz	
	price	prize	

TEST 📼

Listen to these sentences. Circle the word in parentheses that you hear.

1. Do you spell that with a (C/Z)?
2. Do you hear a (bus/buzz)?
3. (Sip/Zip) it slowly.
4. They (race/raise) horses.
5. What's the (price/prize)?

PRACTICE 2 ☐

Listen and repeat:

Zzz!	surprises	is	something's
zoo	Susan	does	contains
buzzing	Liz	says	Jones
surprising	Ms.	noise	isn't
amazing	these	hisses	
buzzes	bees	smells	

DIALOGUE ☐

Surprises in the Post Office

Ms. Valdez: This package smells funny, Liz.
Ms. Jones: Something's written on it.
Ms. Valdez: What does it say?
Ms. Jones: It says: This package contains six mice.
Ms. Valdez: Ugh!
Ms. Jones: Listen! What's in this sack?
Ms. Valdez: It's making a strange hissing sound.
Sack: (hisses) Sssssssssssssss!
Ms. Jones: Susan! It's a sack of snakes!
Ms. Valdez: Oh, it is! I wonder what's in this box, Liz.
Ms. Jones: It's making a buzzing noise.
Box: (buzzes) Zzzzzzzzzzzzzzz!
Ms. Valdez: These are bees!
Ms. Jones: A package of mice! And a sack of snakes! And a box of bees!
This is very surprising.
Ms. Valdez: It's amazing. This isn't a post office, Liz. It's a zoo!

PRONUNCIATION ☐

-s endings

Listen and repeat:

-s = S	-s = Z	-es = IZ
cats	dogs	glasses
snakes	questions	surprises
stamps	parties	boxes
jokes	cars	dishes
sports	things	languages

Now practice these verbs:

likes	wears	watches
hates	loves	washes
speaks	tells	loses
laughs	says	hisses
asks	does	changes

CONVERSATION

Look at the chart below. Then make sentences like the ones in the examples.

Examples:

Susan loves dogs and so does James.
Charles and James wear glasses, and so do I.

	Susan	Liz	Charles	James	You
Loves dogs	X			X	?
Wears glasses			X	X	?
Speaks three languages				X	?
Watches sports	X	X		X	?
Likes parties	X	X	X		?
Hates snakes		X	X		?
Always loses things	X			X	?
Asks a lot of questions	X		X		?
Tells jokes			X	X	?
Loves surprises	X	X	X		?

Note: All -*s* endings follow the same pronunciation rules.

Noun plurals:	cats	dogs	glasses
3rd-person singular present verbs:	likes	wears	watches
Possessives:	Pat's	Susan's	George's
Contraction of is or has:	That's mine.	He's seen it.	Liz's going.*

*Not usually used in writing.

JOINING SOUNDS 📼

The sound z at the end of a word becomes s when the next word begins with s.
Listen and repeat:

loves
She loves surprises.

whose
Whose seat is this?

Sam's
It's Sam's seat.

his
It's his seat.

Who's
Who's speaking to Sam?

SPELLING

The sound z is usually written with the letters z or s.

z, zz, ze	zoo, zipper, dozen, buzz, size, prize
s	easy, busy, reason, cousin, music, visit, present, husband, is, does, has, was, says, words, feels, hears, listens
se	please, these, those, because, exercise, noise, lose, surprise, use (verb), close (verb)

Other spellings:

ss	dessert, scissors, possess
x	(pronounced gz) exam, example, exact, exist

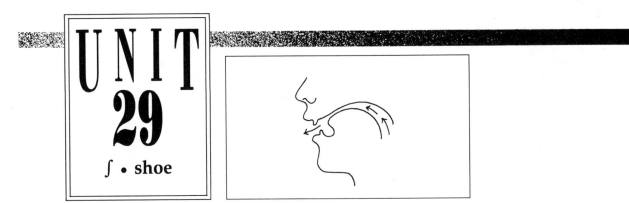

UNIT
29
ʃ • shoe

📼 First practice s.
Then put your tongue up and back a little and push your lips forward a little into
a circle to make ʃ.

PRACTICE 1 🔲

Listen and repeat:

	Sound 1	*Sound 2*	
	Sue	shoe	
	sea	she	
	sip	ship	
	sell	shell	
	lease	leash	

TEST 🔲

Listen to these sentences. Circle the word in parentheses that you hear.

1. Are those (Sue's/shoes)?
2. I'm going to buy some new (seats/sheets).
3. Could you (sign/shine) this, please?
4. Do you have the (lease/leash)?
5. Did you (sell/shell) all the nuts?

PRACTICE 2 ▭

Listen and repeat:

show	sheets	washes	push
shake	shirts	washing machine	Danish
shut	short	Fisher	Swedish
sure	shouldn't	special	washed
sharp	shrink	demonstration	finished

DIALOGUE ▭

A Special Washing Machine

Sally Fisher: Do you sell washing machines?

Sid Sharp: Yes. We're having a special sale on this machine here.

Sally Fisher: Is that a Danish machine? The name looks Danish.

Sid Sharp: No. It's Swedish. Would you like me to demonstrate it for you?

Sally Fisher: Sure. I'd like to see how it washes.

Sid Sharp: OK. Let me give you a demonstration. Here are some sheets and shirts. You put them in the machine. You shut the door. And then you just push this button.

Sally Fisher: The machine shouldn't shake like that, should it?

Sid Sharp: Washing machines always shake. Ah! It's finished.

Sally Fisher: But the sheets have shrunk. And look at how short the shirts are!

Sid Sharp: Oh, those shirts were short before I washed them. And cotton sheets always shrink a little.

Sally Fisher: Well, I'm not sure. Could you show me another machine?

Sid Sharp: Yes, but this is the only machine we have at the special sale price.

JOINING SOUNDS ▭

Listen and repeat:

*Spanish shoes   *Irish shirts

English sheep   *Finnish sheets

British ships   *Danish shrimp

*Swedish shampoo   *Turkish sugar

*French champagne   Swiss chalets

CONVERSATION

Customer: Do you sell Swedish shampoo?

Salesclerk: Yes. We have some Swedish shampoo over there on the shelf.

Practice this conversation. Use the starred (*) words above.

WORD STRESS

Listen and repeat:

Verb	*Noun*
demonstrate	**dem**onstra**tion**
educate	**ed**uca**tion**
operate	**op**era**tion**
	conversa**tion**
	informa**tion**

Words ending in *-ion* have strong stress on the syllable before the *-ion* (exception: **tel**evision).

SPELLING

The sound ∫ is commonly written with the letters *sh*.

    sh   show, shake, sharp, shut, shouldn't, cashier, wash, push, finish

Other spellings:

    ti   vacation, station, information, conversation, education, demonstration, initial, patient

    ci   special, social, official, delicious, especially, musician

    ssi   discussion, profession, permission

    si   pension, dimension

    sci   conscious

    ss   issue, tissue, pressure

    s   sure, sugar, insurance

    ch   machine, chalet, moustache, Chicago

    ce   ocean

    xi   (pronounced k∫) anxious

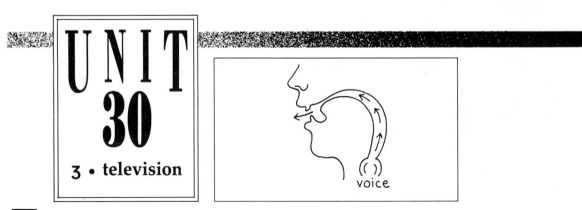

UNIT 30

3 • television

First practice ∫.
Use your voice to make ӡ.

PRACTICE 1 🔲

Listen and repeat:

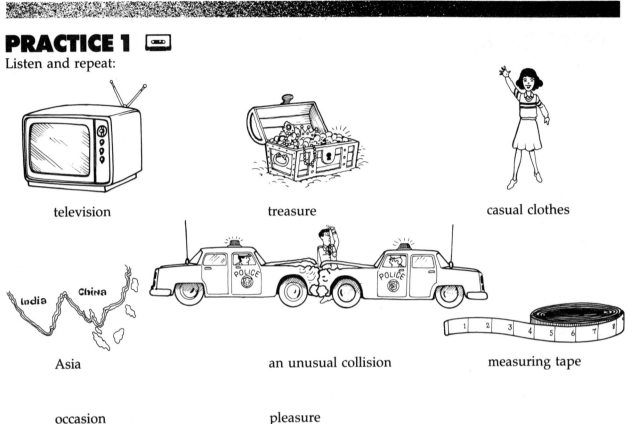

television   treasure   casual clothes

Asia   an unusual collision   measuring tape

occasion   pleasure
invasion   leisurely

READING 🔲

Listen:

Television Tonight on Channel Six

5:00   MOVIE: "Treasure Island"
7:00   LOCAL NEWS: An Unusual Collision
7:15   FASHION: Special Clothes for Casual Occasions
7:30   TRAVEL FILM: A Leisurely Trip Across Asia
8:00   VARIETY SHOW: It's a Pleasure
9:00   DRAMA: Shakespeare's "Measure for Measure"
11:00 SCIENCE FICTION MOVIE: "Invasion of the Martians"

Now read the schedule aloud.

CONVERSATION

Talk about the television programs.

Example:
A: What are you going to watch on television tonight?
B: "Treasure Island."

DRILL 🔳

When somebody says "Thank you" for doing something, we sometimes say, "It was my pleasure" or just "My pleasure." Practice this answer.

Example:

      A: Thank you for lending me your television.
      B: It was my pleasure.

     1. Thank you for fixing my television.
     2. Thanks for lending me *Treasure Island.*
     3. Thanks for lending me your measuring tape.
     4. Thank you for letting me use your garage.
     5. Thanks for letting me drive your Peugeot.

WORD BUILDING 🔳

Listen and repeat:

Verb	*Noun*
in**vade**	in**va**sion
ex**plode**	explo**sion**
de**cide**	de**ci**sion
col**lide**	col**li**sion
di**vide**	di**vi**sion

PRACTICE 2

Read this aloud. Fill in the blanks with the noun related to the underlined verb.

Television News Report

The Secretary of the Treasury has <u>decided</u> to resign. He did not give a reason for his

_____.

A bomb <u>exploded</u> in a parking garage downtown. Two people were injured in the

_____.

There was an unusual _____ tonight. Two police cars <u>collided</u> on Division Avenue.

SPELLING

The sound **3** is usually written with the letters *s* or *ge*.
    s   usually, unusual, measure, leisure, pleasure
    si Asia, Persian, television, occasion, decision
    ge beige, garage,* prestige*
Other spellings:
    ti equation
    z   seizure

*Some people say these words with the sound **d3** instead of **3**.

UNIT 31

tʃ • chair

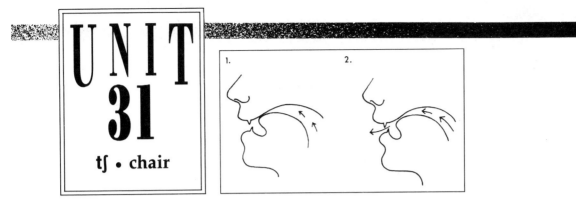

First practice t and ʃ.
Begin to make t.
Then slowly move your tongue away from the roof of your mouth as you say ʃ.

PRACTICE 1

Listen and repeat:

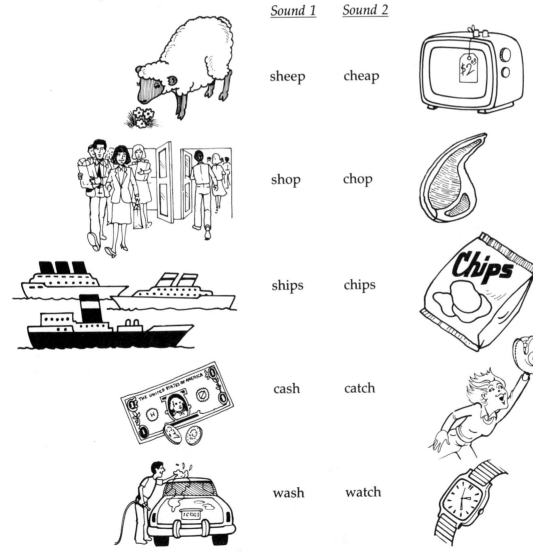

	Sound 1	Sound 2	
	sheep	cheap	
	shop	chop	
	ships	chips	
	cash	catch	
	wash	watch	

TEST 📼

Listen to these sentences. Circle the word in parentheses that you hear.

1. That's a very expensive (shop/chop).
2. I don't like (ships/chips).
3. Are those (sheep/cheap)?
4. Could you (wash/watch) the car for me?
5. He (shows/chose) his paintings at an art gallery.

PRACTICE 2 📼

Listen and repeat:

check	which	butcher shop
choose	much	shoulder chops
cheapest	lunch	the children's lunch
Ms. Chan	church	a delicious chicken

DIALOGUE 📼

At the Butcher Shop

Butcher: Good morning, Ms. Chan. What can I get you today?
Ms. Chan: Good morning, Mr. Church. I'd like some lamb chops for the children's lunch.
Butcher: Shoulder chops, Ms. Chan?
Ms. Chan: Yes. I'll take four shoulder chops and I'd like a small chicken.
Butcher: Would you like to choose a chicken?
Ms. Chan: Which one is cheaper?
Butcher: This one's the cheapest.
Ms. Chan: How much is all that? I don't have much cash. Can I give you a check?
Butcher: Yes, of course, Ms. Chan.

RECIPE 📼
Cheese-Topped Chops

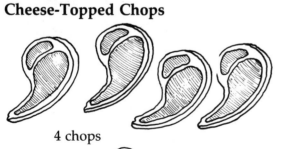

4 chops

chicken broth

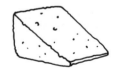

cheddar cheese

mushrooms

shallots

1 fresh chili pepper (chopped)

or a pinch of chili powder
(not too much chili)

1. Pour a little chicken broth over the chops.

2. Chop the mushrooms, shallots, and cheese.

3. Mix the mushrooms, shallots, cheese, and chili in a bowl.

4. Broil the chops.

5. Put the chops in a dish.

6. Spread the cheese mixture over the chops.

7. Broil the chops and cheese mixture for a few minutes.

8. Serve the chops with French bread and a fresh spinach and mushroom salad.

CONVERSATION

Imagine that you are having guests for dinner.
In a group of four or five people, plan the meal you will serve.
Each dish should include a food with the ʃ or tʃ sound in it.

SPELLING

The sound tʃ is usually written with the letters *ch* or *tch*.

　　ch　cheap, chicken, cheese, children, teacher, which, much
　　tch　kitchen, match, watch, butcher, catch

Other spellings:

　　t　(before *u*) picture, mixture, literature, century, future, actual, natural
　　ti　(after *s*) question, suggestion
　　c　cello, concerto

UNIT 32

dʒ • joke

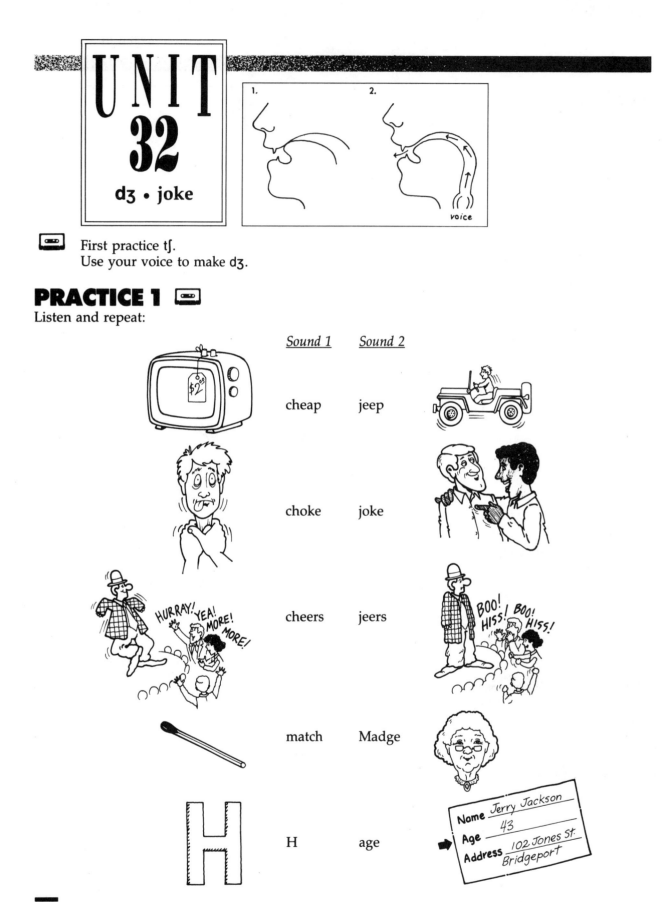

First practice tʃ.
Use your voice to make dʒ.

PRACTICE 1

Listen and repeat:

	Sound 1	_Sound 2_	
	cheap	jeep	
	choke	joke	
	cheers	jeers	
	match	Madge	
	H	age	

TEST

Listen to these sentences. Circle the word in parentheses that you hear.

1. I'm (choking/joking).
2. Are those (cherries/Jerry's)?
3. The crowd (cheered/jeered) when he spoke.
4. They didn't say their (H's/ages).
5. Are these (matches/Madge's)?

PRACTICE 2 □

Listen and repeat:

just	dangerous	village
jeep	manager	bridge
January	agency	edge
Jerry	injured	large
jokes	passenger	Bridgeport
jail	damaged	George Churchill

DIALOGUE □

George Churchill

Jerry: Just outside this village there's a very dangerous bridge.
John: Yes. Charlie told me two jeeps crashed there in January. Did you hear how it happened?
Jerry: Well, George Churchill was driving the larger jeep. He was driving very dangerously.
John: George Churchill. Do I know George Churchill?
Jerry: Yes, I think you do. He's the manager of the travel agency in Bridgeport.
John: Oh, yes. I remember George. He's always telling jokes. Well, was anybody injured?
Jerry: Oh, yes. The other jeep went over the edge of the bridge, and two children and another passenger were badly injured.
John: Were both jeeps damaged?
Jerry: Oh, yes.
John: And what happened to George?
Jerry: George? He's telling jokes in jail now, I suppose!

JOINING SOUNDS □

When two sounds tʃ or dʒ come together, say both sounds. Listen and repeat:

orange juice	rich children	which job
a large jeep	a watch chain	large cherries
the village jail	which chair	teach German
change jobs	how much cheese	

Crossword

Every answer has the sound tʃ or dʒ.

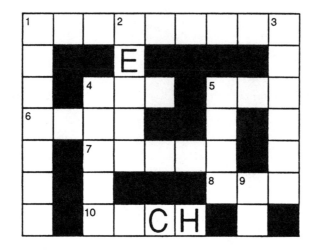

Clues

Across:
1 Famous English prime minister.
4 I put butter and _____ on my bread.
5 You buy jam in a _____.
6 You'll get fat if you eat too much _____olate.
7 The past tense of *choose* is _____.
8 An open room on the outside of a house is a _____ch.
10 This isn't _____ a difficult puzzle.

Down:
1 A hen is a female _____.
2 Could you get me the book on the top shelf? I'm not tall enough to _____ it.
3 George's jeep was _____ than the other jeep.
4 This book belongs to Jock. It's _____' book.
5 George Churchill was driving a _____.
9 Tell me a funny j_____e.

SPELLING

The sound dʒ is usually written with the letters *j* or *g*.

    j   job, just, joke, January, June, jail, injure, enjoy, subject
    g   (before *e, i,* or *y*) general, dangerous, agency, suggest, passenger, engine, original, energy, biology, gym
    ge   village, large, orange, age, average, college, language
   dge bridge, edge, judge, knowledge
    dj   adjective, adjust
Other spellings:
    d   (before *u* or *i*) educate, graduate, gradual, individual, procedure, soldier

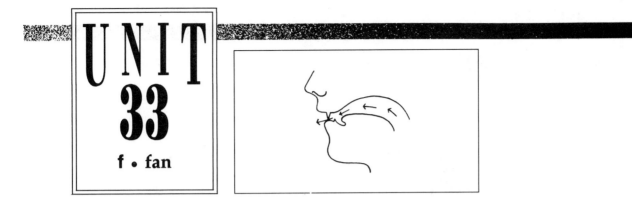

Touch your top teeth with your bottom lip.
Blow out air between your lip and your teeth.

PRACTICE 1

Listen and repeat:

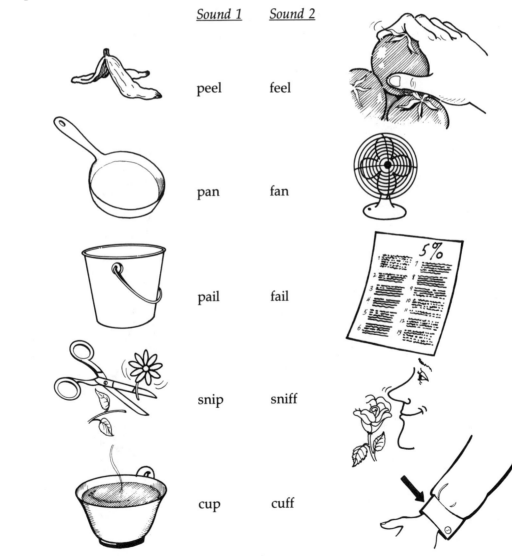

	Sound 1	_Sound 2_
	peel	feel
	pan	fan
	pail	fail
	snip	sniff
	cup	cuff

PRACTICE 2 🔲

Listen and repeat:

	Sound 1	*Sound 2*	
	hill	fill	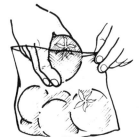
	heel	feel	
	hat	fat	
	heat	feet	
	hall	fall	

TEST 🔲

Listen to these sentences. Circle the word in parentheses that you hear.

1. (Peel/Feel) this orange.
2. Could you (hold/fold) this sweater?
3. This (cup/cuff) is dirty.
4. I bought a new (pan/fan).
5. They met in the (hall/fall).
6. (Hey!/Fay!) Look at this!

PRACTICE 3 🔲

Listen and repeat:

funny	friendly	phone	comfortable
five	finished	photograph	laugh
form	Fran	photographer	wife
front	Fred Fuller	profile	myself
first	prefer	cheerful	
February	office	difficult	

DIALOGUE 🔲

At the Photographer's

Fred:	I want a photograph of myself and my wife.
Photographer:	Fill out this form, please.
	Would you prefer a front photograph or a profile?
Fred:	A front photograph, don't you think, Fran?
Fran:	Yes. Front.
Photographer:	Please sit on this sofa. Are you comfortable?
Fran:	Yes. This is fine.
Photographer:	Mr. Fuller, give a happy laugh.
Fred:	That's difficult. If you say something funny, I'll laugh.
Photographer:	And, Mrs. Fuller, please look cheerful and friendly.
Fred:	(laughs)
Fran:	Finished?
Photographer:	Yes.
Fred:	Will the photograph be ready the first of February?
Photographer:	Yes. Phone my office in five days.
Fred:	Fine.

INTONATION 🔲

Listen and repeat:

If Fred **laughs**, he looks **funny**.

If Grandfather **flies**, he gets **fright**ened.

JUMBLED SENTENCES

Match words from the left column with words from the right column.

Example:

If Fred laughs, he looks funny.

If Fred laughs,	don't forget to buy fish.
If Fran laughs,	he gets frightened.
If Grandfather flies,	call the telephone operator.
If you buy fish,	she looks friendly.
If you need information,	I'll feel better.
If you fry all your food,	make sure it's fresh.
If I feel better on Friday,	you'll get fat.
If you're going shopping,	he looks funny.
If I get some fresh air,	I'll go to my friend's party.

SPELLING

The sound f is usually written with the letter *f*.

f   fifty, fine, first, finish, front, funny, friendly, February, prefer, before, cheerful, often, self, life, wife

ff   off, office, coffee, difficult, different, sniff, cuff

Other spellings:

ph   telephone, photograph, paragraph, philosophy, hyphen

gh   laugh, enough, rough, cough, tough

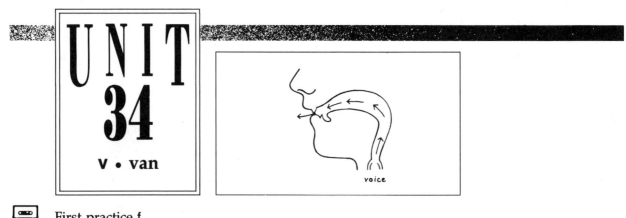

UNIT 34
v • van

voice

First practice f.
Use your voice to make v.

PRACTICE 1 📼

Listen and repeat:

	Sound 1	_Sound 2_	
	fan	van	
	fine	vine	
	few	view	
	leaf	leave	
	half	halve	

PRACTICE 2 ▭

Listen and repeat:

	Sound 1	Sound 2	
	ban	van	
	B	V	
	best	vest	
	boat	vote	
	cabs	calves	

TEST ▭

Listen to these sentences. Circle the word in parentheses that you hear.

1. Is this the (best/vest)?
2. One person – one (boat/vote).
3. This room has a (few/view).
4. The (fan/van) isn't working.
5. (Half/Halve) the apple.
6. Have you seen any (cabs/calves)?

PRACTICE 3 📼

Listen and repeat:

very	Victor	waving	love
village	view	Vivian	lovely
valley	living	have	moved
van	November	of	lived
vine	driving	five	leaves

DIALOGUE 📼

A View of the Valley

Vivian: Has your family lived here for very long?
Victor: Five and a half years. We moved here on the first of November.
Vivian: You have a fantastic view.
Victor: Yes. I love living here.
Vivian: Look! You can see the village way down in the valley.
Victor: Yes. It's a lovely view.

READING

Read this aloud. Choose the words that describe the picture.

    √   This is a picture of a farmer (arriving at/leaving) a village in the (forest/valley). He's driving a (bus/van) and (waving/laughing) at a friend. It's a fine (evening/afternoon), but it's November, and the leaves have fallen from the √ (vine/fir tree) in the front of the picture. There are (four/five) leaves on the ground.

RELATED WORDS ENDING IN *f* AND *v*

Nouns ending in the sound f often change the *f* to *v* in the plural. Listen:

Singular	*Plural*
leaf	leaves
wife	wives
life	lives
calf	calves
knife	knives

Nouns ending in *f* often have related verbs that end in the sound v.

Noun	*Verb*
belief	believe
proof	prove
half	halve
life	live

SPELLING

The sound v is written with the letter *v:*

    v very, visit, valley, view, November, seven, over, never, river, every
        give,* have,* live,* twelve,* love,* move,* drive*

Other spellings:

    f of

*English words do not end in the letter *v*. Words that end with the sound v always add the letter *e* in the spelling.

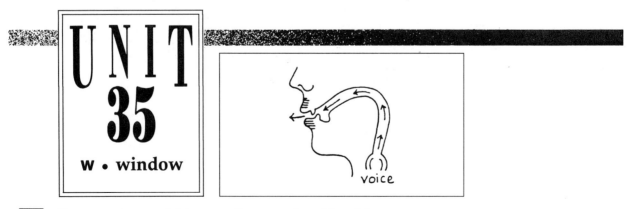

UNIT
35
w • window

voice

First practice uw. Make your lips round and hard for w.
w is a short sound.

PRACTICE 1 🔊

Listen and repeat:

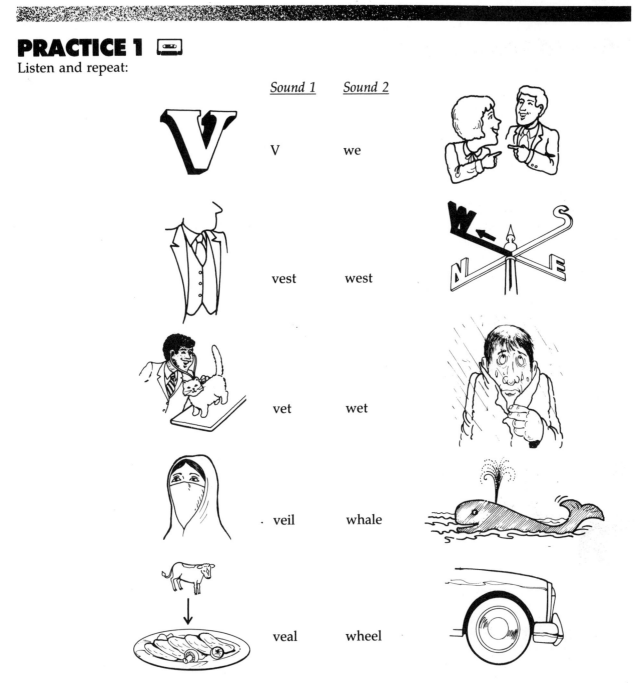

	Sound 1	Sound 2
	V	we
	vest	west
	vet	wet
	veil	whale
	veal	wheel

TEST 🔊

Listen to these sentences. Circle the word in parentheses that you hear.

1. Does this say ("V"/"we")?
2. Look for it in the (vest/west).
3. The (veils/whales) were gray.
4. Is this book (verse/worse)?
5. There's something wrong with this (veal/wheel).

113

PRACTICE 2 [cassette]

Listen and repeat:

windy	warm	what	twelve
wasn't	wore	when	twenty
Wednesday	were	everywhere	quiet
walk	wonderful	anyway	quickly
Wendy went	wool	sandwiches	squirrels
we watched	woods	sweaters	

DIALOGUE [cassette]

A Walk in the Woods

Vera: Did you see Victor on Wednesday, Wendy?

Wendy: Yes. We went for a walk in the woods near the highway.

Vera: Wasn't it cold on Wednesday?

Wendy: Yes. It was very cold and windy. We wore heavy wool sweaters and walked quickly to keep warm.

Vera: It's so nice and quiet in the woods.

Wendy: Yes. Farther away from the highway it was very quiet and there were birds and squirrels everywhere. We counted over twenty squirrels.

Vera: It sounds wonderful. Did you take lunch with you?

Wendy: Yes. We brought veal sandwiches. We stopped around twelve, and we ate and watched the squirrels, but it was too windy to sit long. It was a very nice walk, anyway.

INTONATION [cassette]

Statements and wh-questions end with a falling tone. Make sure your voice rises on the last stressed syllable and then falls.

Listen and repeat:

Who went for a **walk**?   Wendy and **Vic**tor.

Where was it **quiet**?   In the **woods**.

When did Wendy see **Vic**tor?   On **Wednes**day.

JUMBLED ANSWERS

Ask and answer questions. Work in pairs. Person A should cover person B's column with a piece of paper, and B should cover A's column.

_A_	_B_
What did Wendy and Victor do on Wednesday?	Veal sandwiches.
Where did they walk?	The squirrels.
What did they watch?	In the woods.
Where were the squirrels?	To keep warm.
Why did they walk quickly?	Twelve o'clock.
What did they bring to eat?	In the woods.
What time did they have lunch?	Heavy wool sweaters.
What did they wear?	They went for a walk.

SPELLING

The sound **w** is usually written with the letter *w*:

w   walk, water, wear, warm, winter, woods, woman, twenty,
sweater

Other spellings:

wh*   what, when, where, which, why, while, white, whisper, whether,
everywhere

u   (after *q* or sometimes *g* or *s*) question, quiet, quickly, square, squirrel
language, persuade

o   one, once, everyone

*Many people say these words with the sound **hw**.

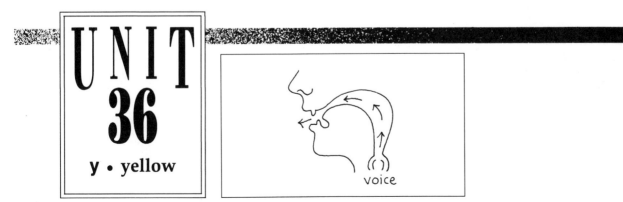

U N I T
36
y • yellow

voice

First practice **iy**.
Very quickly move your tongue to make the next sound.
Do not touch the roof of your mouth with your tongue.

PRACTICE 1 🔲

Listen and repeat:

	Sound 1	Sound 2	
	joke	yolk	
	jam	yam	
	jail	Yale	
	jeers	years	
	Jess	yes	

TEST

Listen to these sentences. Circle the word in parentheses that you hear.

1. Their son went to (jail/Yale).
2. Did you taste the (jam/yam)?
3. That's a bad (joke/yolk).
4. The (jeers/years) were painful for him.
5. (Jess/Yes), let's go to the movies.

PRACTICE 2

Listen and repeat:

yes	used to	few	millionaire
yesterday	excuse me	familiar	university
yellow	music	peculiar	NYU*
years	musician	opinion	Hugh Young
you	computer	interview	Houston
uses (noun)	future	executive	huge

*NYU = New York University

DIALOGUE

A Music Student

Yoko: Excuse me. You look familiar. Did you use to live in New York?
Jack: Yes.
Yoko: Did you use to work at NYU?
Jack: Yes. I taught music there for a few years.
Yoko: Oh. Did you know Hugh Young? He was a music student.
Jack: Hugh Young? Didn't he use to wear a funny yellow jacket all the time?
Yoko: Yes. And he used to play the piano with a jazz group at the university.
Jack: Yes, I remember Hugh. Most people thought he was a little...uh...
         peculiar. Do you know what he's doing now?
Yoko: Yes. He's a millionaire in Houston now.
Jack: A millionaire? As a jazz musician?
Yoko: Oh, no. He's an executive for a huge computer company. I saw an
         interview with him on TV yesterday. They were asking his opinion
         about future uses for computers.
Jack: Well! I guess people don't find him so peculiar anymore.

PRONUNCIATION

Listen and repeat:

used to
He used to play the piano.
Did you use to live in New York?

used to and *use to* are both pronounced **yuw**stə.

117

CONVERSATION

Practice in pairs.

Example: play the piano
      A: When you were younger, did you use to play the piano?
      B: Yes, I did.   /   No, I didn't.

   1. like music

   2. enjoy school

   3. listen to your parents

   4. argue with your brothers or sisters

   5. wear a uniform to school

   6. tell jokes

   7. be very curious

   8. think about your future

SPELLING

The sound y is usually written with the letter *y*. The sound y is also often part of the spelling *u*.

   y   yes, you, yesterday, young, yellow, year, beyond
   u   (1) at the beginning of a word: use, university, usually (but not in the prefix
         un: unhappy)
         (2) after the consonant sounds p, b, m, f, v, k, g, h: computer, ambulance,
         music, communication, future, confuse, cute, excuse, executive, argue,
         human, humor, huge (but not after the letter *q*)
         (3) in the middle of a word: also after the consonants n and l, if the *u* vowel
         does not have strong stress: January, annual, continue, menu, value,
         volume

Other spellings:
   i   familiar, millionaire, opinion, brilliant, peculiar, convenient
   ew, iew   (pronounced yuw) few, view, review, interview
   eau   (pronounced yuw) beautiful

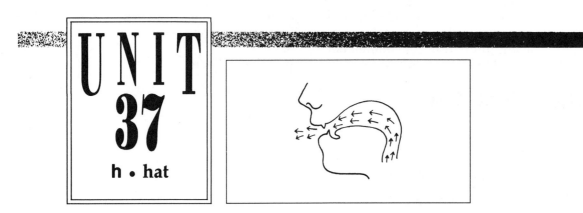

UNIT
37
h • hat

Push a lot of air out very quickly.
Do not touch the roof of your mouth with your tongue.

PRACTICE 1

Listen and repeat:

	Sound 1 *(no sound)*	*Sound 2*	
	ill	hill	
	eat	heat	
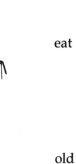	old	hold	
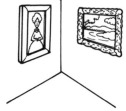	art	heart	
	eye	high	

TEST

Listen to these sentences. Circle the word in parentheses that you hear.

1. Did you (eat/heat) the soup?
2. It was (I/high).
3. What nice, clean (air/hair)!
4. I (ate/hate) eggs for breakfast.
5. Is this (art/heart)?

PRACTICE 2 🔲

Listen and repeat:

hello	happen	hospital	hope
hit	husband	Hilda Harris	behind
house	having	heard	Helen
hurt	horrible	home	unhappy

DIALOGUE 🔲

A Horrible Accident

Helen: Hello, Ellen.

Ellen: Hello, Helen. Have you heard the news? There's been a horrible accident.

Helen: Oh, no! What happened?

Ellen: Hilda Harris's husband, Henry, had an accident on his way home from work.

Helen: How awful! Was he hurt?

Ellen: Yes. He was taken to the hospital in an ambulance.

Helen: How did it happen?

Ellen: His car was hit by an express train. It happened at the crossing just behind his house.

Helen: How horrible!

Ellen: He's having an operation in the hospital now. Poor Hilda! You can imagine how unhappy she is.

Helen: I hope he'll be all right.

Ellen: I hope so, too.

Note: The sound h is often dropped in unstressed words like *he* or *his* (but not at the beginning of a sentence).

INTONATION 🔲

Listen and repeat:

Oh, **no**!   How **horrible**!

How **awful**!   How **terrible**!

CONVERSATION

Practice in pairs. Fill in the blanks with a word or phrase from the columns below.

Example:

A: Have you heard about *Henry* ?   [column 1]

B: No. What happened?

A: *He had an accident* .   [column 2]

B: *How awful* !   [column 3]

Substitute:

<u>1</u>	<u>2</u>	<u>3</u>
Howard	He had an accident.	Oh, no!
Alan	A helicopter hit his house.	How awful!
Henry	He has a hole in his head.	How horrible!
Hilda	She hit herself with a hammer.	How terrible!
Helen's father	He had a heart attack.	
Ellen's husband	He had to be taken to the hospital.	
Harry	He hurt both his hands and can't hold anything.	

READING

Fill in the blanks using these words. You can use some words more than once.

he   happy
have   unhappy
hurt   hospital
him

An old man is very sick and goes into the _____ to

_____ an operation. _____ is very _____

and afraid. When _____ arrives at the _____,

a nurse gives _____ a bath. After the bath, _____ is

very _____ and _____ says to the nurse, "I was very

afraid to _____ that operation, but it didn't _____

me at all."

SPELLING

The sound h is usually spelled with the letter h:
   h   how, help, head, heart, hope, happy, unhappy, hospital, behind, human
       hothouse, penthouse, uphill
Other spellings:
   wh   who, whose, whom, whole
The letter h is silent in:
   hour, honest, honor, heir, oh, John, vehicle, exhaust, rhyme,
   shepherd, silhouette

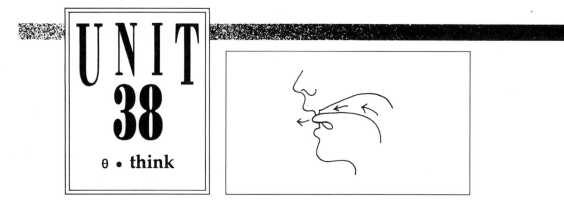

U N I T 38

θ • think

Put your tongue between your teeth.
Blow out air between your tongue and top teeth.

PRACTICE 1

Listen and repeat:

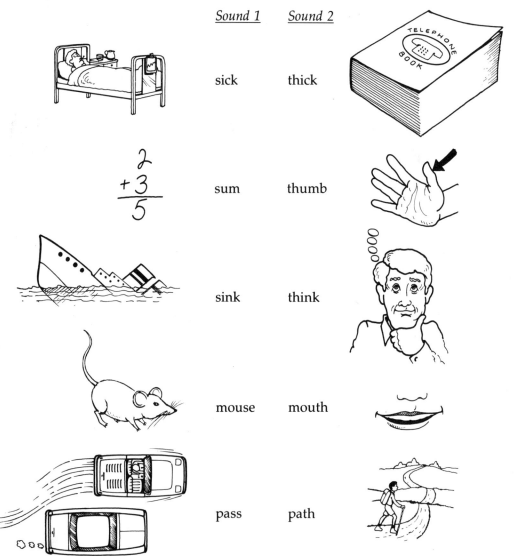

	Sound 1	*Sound 2*	
	sick	thick	
	sum	thumb	
	sink	think	
	mouse	mouth	
	pass	path	

PRACTICE 2 📼

Listen and repeat:

		Sound 1	_Sound 2_	

 first   thirst

 free   three

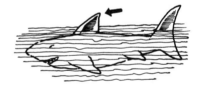 fin   thin

 Fred   thread

roof   Ruth

123

PRACTICE 3 🖭

Listen and repeat:

	Sound 1	*Sound 2*	
	tie	thigh	
	tree	three	
	tanks	thanks	
	bat	bath	
	tent	tenth	

TEST 📼

Listen to these sentences. Circle the word in parentheses that you hear.

1. It's very (sick/thick).
2. Send (tanks/thanks).
3. She (taught/thought) for a long time.
4. This (bat/bath) is too small.
5. I always (sink/think) in the pool.
6. Do you want these (free/three) books?

PRACTICE 4 📼

Listen and repeat:

thank you	thousand	anything	worth
thought	three hundred	something	Edith Roth
thirsty	Theodore	birthday	month
Thursday	author	mathematician	Roths'
thirty-three	Arthur	Judith	moths

DIALOGUE 📼

Gossips

Judith: Edith Roth is thirty.
Arthur: Is she? I thought she was thirty-three.
Judith: Her birthday was last Thursday.
Arthur: Was it? I thought it was last month.
Judith: The Roths' house is worth $300,000.
Arthur: Is it? I thought it was worth about $30,000.
Judith: Theodore Roth is the author of a book about moths.
Arthur: Is he? I thought he was a mathematician.
Judith: I'm so thirsty.
Arthur: Are you? I thought you had something to drink at the Roths'.
Judith: No. Edith didn't give me anything to drink.
Arthur: I'll buy you a drink.
Judith: Oh! Thank you.

STRESS 📼

Listen and repeat:

Is she? I thought she was thirty-**three**.
Was it? I thought it was last **month**.
Is it? I thought it was worth about **thir**ty thousand.
Are you? I thought you **drank** something.

JUMBLED SENTENCES

Do this in pairs. A should cover B's sentences with a piece of paper, and B should cover A's sentences.

Example:

A: Judith is at the theater.

B: Is she? I thought she was at the Roths'.

A: Judith is at the theater.
The Roths' house is north of here.
It's Edith's birthday today.
I'm so thirsty.
Theodore is thirty-three.
The Roths' house is worth $300,000.
The math test is Tuesday.

B: Is it? I thought it was last month.
Is she? I thought she was at the Roths'.
Are you? I thought you just drank something.
Is it? I thought it was south.
Is it? I thought it was worth $30,000.
Is he? I thought he was thirty.
Is it? I thought it was on Thursday.

SPELLING

The sound θ is spelled with the letters *th:*

th think, thirty, thousand, thick, thin, thought, thirsty, Thursday, through, author, nothing, birthday, month, mouth, fourth, fifth, both, north, south, truth, warmth, length, strength, worth, healthy

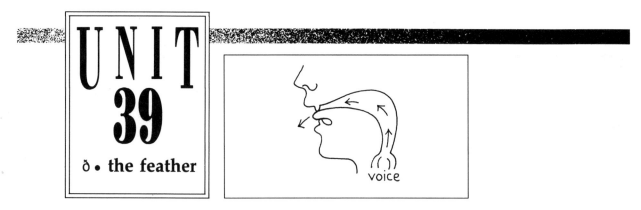

UNIT 39
ð • the feather

voice

First practice θ. Use your voice to make ð.

PRACTICE 1 📼

Listen and repeat:

Sound 1   _Sound 2_

day   they

dare   there

doze   those

Dan   than

side   scythe

127

PRACTICE 2

Practice these questions and answers:

What's this?  This is a zoo.

What are those? Those are zebras.

What's this? This is a Z.

What's that? That's a zero.

What are these? These are zippers.

Who's that?  That's Zack.

PRACTICE 3

Listen and repeat:

	Sound 1	*Sound 2*	
	bays	bathe	
	breeze	breathe	
	tease	teethe	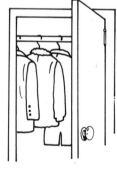
	closing	clothing	
	size	scythe	

129

TEST

Listen to these sentences. Circle the word in parentheses that you hear.

1. (Day/They) finally came.
2. (Dave/They've) left.
3. The child was just (teasing/teething).
4. Try to pronounce (D's/Z's/these) more clearly.
5. Is it (closing/clothing)?

PRACTICE 4

Listen and repeat:

the	together	leather	Heather
this	feathers	smoother	clothes*
that	another	rather	
there	the other	either	

*Many people pronounce clothes like "cloze."

DIALOGUE 📼

The Hat in the Window

Heather: I'd like to buy the hat in the window.
Salesclerk: There are three hats together in the window, Madam. Do you want the one with the feathers?
Heather: No. The other one.
Salesclerk: The small one for thirteen dollars?
Heather: No. Not that one either. That one over there. The leather one.
Salesclerk: Ah! The leather one. Now here's another leather hat. This one is better than the one in the window. It's a smoother leather.
Heather: I'd rather have the one in the window. The color goes better with my clothes.
Salesclerk: Certainly, Madam, if that's the one you want. But we don't take anything out of the window until three o'clock on Thursday.

STRESS 📼

Listen and repeat:

Which jacket do you **think** is **bet**ter than the **oth**ers?
I think the **one** with the **belt** is **bet**ter than the **oth**ers.

CONVERSATION

Talk about the three jackets using words from the list below.

A: Which jacket do you think is . . . than the others?
B: I think the | one with the belt | is | . . . than the others.
                | leather jacket | looks |
                | short jacket for $36 | |

better	more **prac**tical	**nic**er	more **styl**ish
warmer	more **at**tractive	**dress**ier	more **cas**ual
cheaper	more **com**fortable		

SPELLING

The sound ð is written with the letters *th:*

th   this, that, there, though, mother, father, brother, weather, leather, rather,
either, another, together, clothes, smooth

Look at the spellings for these words with the sounds θ and ð:

θ   bath, breath, teeth, cloth (nouns)
north, south, worth

ð   bathe, breathe, teethe, clothe (verbs)
northern, southern, worthy

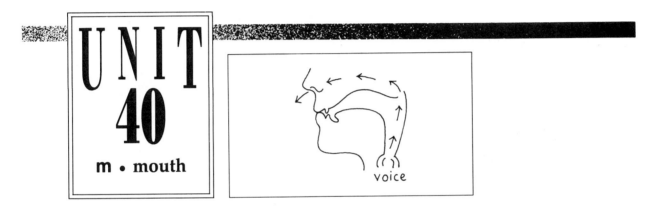

UNIT 40
m • mouth

voice

Close your lips.
Use your voice.
m comes through your nose.

PRACTICE 1

Listen and repeat:

Mm!	tomorrow	Jim	smart
met	summer	time	Mrs. Smith
maybe	family	come	homemade
muffins	remember	home	Tom Mitchum
Maine	Mom	small	Mm?

DIALOGUE

Mom's Muffins

Jim:	Mom?
Mrs. Smith:	Mm?
Jim:	Can my friend, Tom Mitchum, come home with me for lunch tomorrow?
Mrs. Smith:	Of course, Jim. Have I met Tom before?
Jim:	Mm-hmm. You met him last summer. He's small and very smart.
Mrs. Smith:	Oh, yes. I remember Tom. His family comes from Maine, right?
Jim:	Yes. Oh, um, Mom? Will you make some homemade muffins tomorrow?
Mrs. Smith:	Mm . . . maybe. If I have time.
Jim:	I told Tom about your muffins, Mom. That's why he's coming for lunch tomorrow!

INTONATION 📼

"Mm" has many meanings. Practice these:

⌣
Mm means "What did you say?"

⌢
Mm means "Yes."

∿
Mmmm means "This is good!" (or "nice" or "delicious").

Now listen to this conversation and say which meaning "Mm" has in B's answers.

A: Would you like some homemade muffins?
B: Mm?
A: Would you like some muffins?
B: Mm.
A: Here you are.
B: (*eating*) Mm!
A: I'm glad you like them. I made them myself. Would you like to try them with marmalade?
B: Mm?
A: Marmalade. They're marvelous with marmalade. Would you like some?
B: Mm.
A: Here you are.
B: (*eating*) Mm!

SPELLING

The sound m is written with the letter *m:*

m   maybe, family, remember, tomorrow, time, some, homemade, small, from
mm   summer
         swim – swimming

Other spellings:
mb   (*b* is silent) comb, lamb, climb, bomb, thumb
mn   (*n* is silent) autumn, column

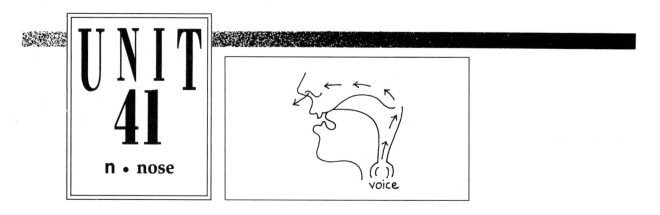

UNIT 41
n • nose

📼 Put your tongue on the roof of your mouth.
     Touch your side teeth with the sides of your tongue.
     Use your voice. n comes through your nose.

PRACTICE 1

Listen and repeat:

	Sound 1	Sound 2	
	me	knee	
	mine	nine	
	comb	cone	
	gum	gun	
	name	mane	

TEST

Listen to these sentences. Circle the word in parentheses that you hear.

1. I'll give you (mine/nine).
2. I'd like two (combs/cones), please.
3. I think they're (mice/nice).
4. Be careful – don't step on the (gum/gun)!
5. What a beautiful (name/mane)!

PRACTICE 2 🔲

Listen and repeat:

noise	midnight	tenant	don't
rent	inexpensive	friends	can't
an apartment	unfurnished	landlord	$599
downtown	twenty	month	
often	prison	garden	didn't
oven	station	forbidden	
Seventh Avenue	television	Tony Martin	
11:15	kitchen	certainly	

DIALOGUE 🔲

At a Rental Agency

Tony Martin: Good morning. I'm looking for a one-bedroom apartment downtown.

Rental Agent: Certainly, sir. How much rent did you want to pay?

Tony Martin: Well, I didn't want to pay more than $520 a month.

Rental Agent: $520 a month? We don't often have apartments as inexpensive as that. We have one apartment for $599 a month, on Seventh Avenue. It's near the station.

Tony Martin: Is it furnished?

Rental Agent: No. It's unfurnished. It has a kitchen, but no oven. There's a garden in the back, but the tenants can't use it. The landlord lives downstairs. Friends are forbidden in the apartment after midnight. No noise and no television after 11:15. No...

Tony Martin: No, thank you! I want an apartment, not a prison!

GAME

Mini-Bingo

1	7	11	9	10	13	17	15	18	19
20	21	22	23	24	25	26	27	28	29
70	71	72	73	74	75	76	77	78	79
90	91	92	93	94	95	96	97	98	99

Play in a group of five people. One person calls out the numbers above in any order.

The others each choose one of the boxes A, B, C, or D.

Cross out each number in your box as it is called (or put a small piece of paper on top of each number as it is called).

The first person to cross out all the numbers in one box wins.

A

9	20	99
15	79	71
97	19	10

B

1	79	11
13	9	7
99	27	10

C

77	79	99
18	19	97
11	91	29

D

1	79	9
17	19	18
99	21	70

SPELLING

The sound n is spelled with the letter *n:*

   n   name, number, ninety, apartment, tenant, didn't, none, person

   nn penny, funny, sunny, dinner

       run – running, begin – beginner, beginning, thin – thinner

Other spellings:

   kn know, knife, knee, knock

   gn foreign, sign, design, campaign

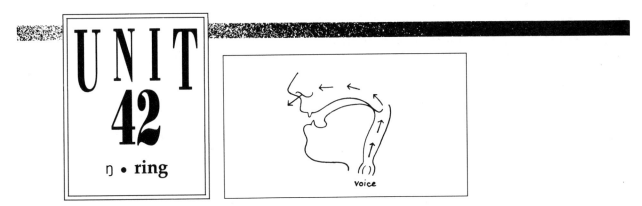

UNIT 42
ŋ • ring

Touch the back of the roof of your mouth with the back of your tongue.
Use your voice. ŋ comes through your nose.

PRACTICE 1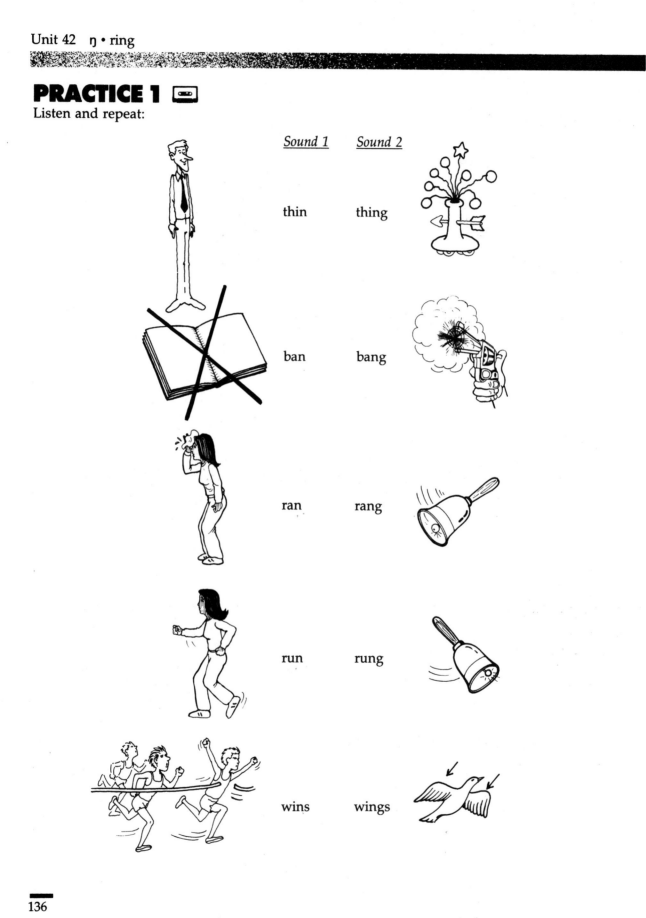

Listen and repeat:

	Sound 1	_Sound 2_	
	thin	thing	
	ban	bang	
	ran	rang	
	run	rung	
	wins	wings	

PRACTICE 2

Listen and repeat:

	Sound 1	*Sound 2*	
	think	thing	
	bank	bang	
	sink	sing	
	rink	ring	
	winks	wings	

137

TEST 📼

Listen to these sentences. Circle the word in parentheses that you hear.

1. I couldn't find the (rink/ring).
2. He (banned/banged) the book.
3. Tony always (sinks/sings) in the pool.
4. You should (ban/bank/bang) it.
5. This is not the right place for (sinners/sinkers/singers).

PRACTICE 3 📼

Listen and repeat:

pink	morning	strong string	ringing
drink	something	standing	bringing
finger	Mr. King	happening	singing
angrily	Mrs. Singer	running	banging
			hanging

DIALOGUE 📼

Noisy Neighbors

Mr. Singer: (angrily) Bang! Bang! Bang! What are the Kings doing at seven o'clock on Sunday morning?

Mrs. Singer: Well, Mr. King is singing.

Mr. Singer: Yes, but what's the banging noise?

Mrs. Singer: (looking out the window) He's standing on a ladder and banging some nails into the wall with a hammer. Now he's hanging some strong string on the nails.

Mr. Singer: And what's Mrs. King doing?

Mrs. Singer: She's bringing something pink for Mr. King to drink. Now she's putting it . . . Oh!

Mr. Singer: What's happening?

Mrs. Singer: The ladder's falling.

Mr. Singer: What's Mr. King doing?

Mrs. Singer: He's hanging from the string. He's holding onto the string with his fingers and shouting to Mrs. King.

Mr. Singer: And is she helping him?

Mrs. Singer: No. She's running toward our house. That's her ringing the bell.

Mr. Singer: Well, I'm not going to answer it. I'm sleeping.

CONVERSATION

Talk about these pictures.

Example: Mrs. Singer

What's Mrs. Singer doing?
She's looking out the window.

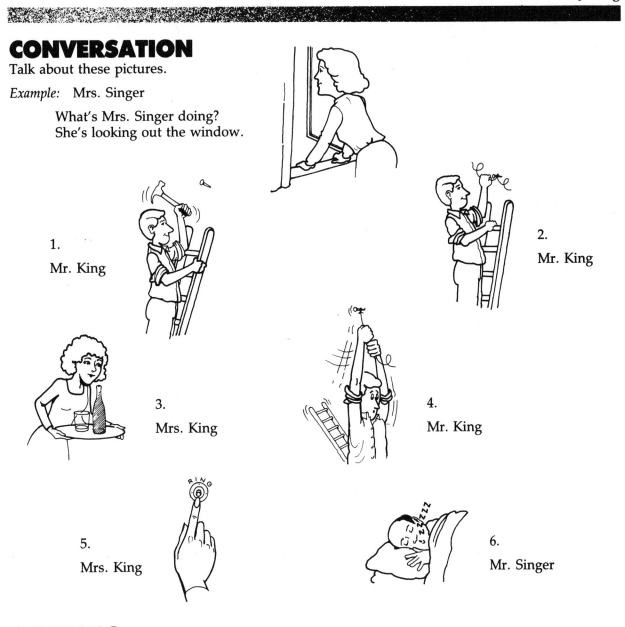

1.
Mr. King

2.
Mr. King

3.
Mrs. King

4.
Mr. King

5.
Mrs. King

6.
Mr. Singer

SPELLING

The sound ŋ is usually written with the letters *ng:*

ng   morning, ring, singing, singer, spring, wrong, tongue, long, strong,
young

The sound ŋ is spelled with the letter *n* before a k or g sound:

think, sink, drank, bank, monkey, uncle, ankle
anger, angrily, hunger, hungry, finger, language, English, single, longer,
stronger, younger

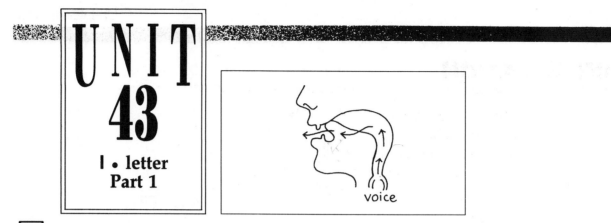

UNIT
43

l • letter
Part 1

voice

First practice n.
To make l, the air goes over the sides of your tongue and out of your mouth.

PRACTICE 1

Listen and repeat:

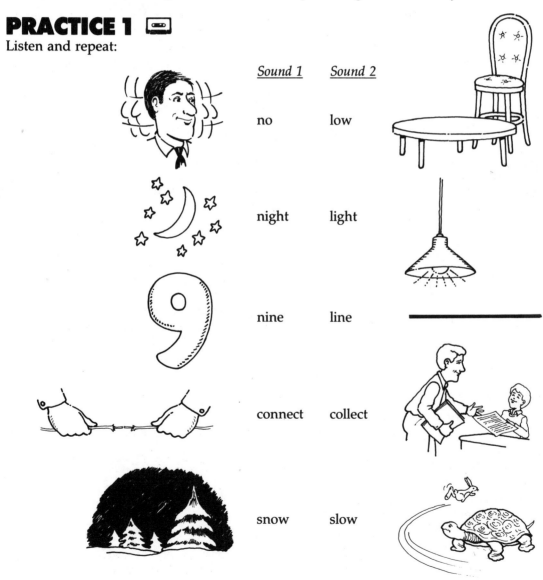

Sound 1	*Sound 2*
no	low
night	light
nine	line
connect	collect
snow	slow

TEST

Listen to these sentences. Circle the word in parentheses that you hear.

1. Write it under the (nine/line).
2. There were (no/low) tables in the room.
3. Could you (connect/collect) these?
4. He threw a (snowball/slow ball).
5. Is it (night/light) already?

PRACTICE 2

Listen and repeat:

Now answer these questions.

Who's late for lunch?
What is Ms. Lee doing?
What's on the plate?
Is there a lot of lemonade left or only a little?
What else is left?
Why is Ms. Lee complaining?

PRACTICE 3

Listen and repeat:

Now answer these questions.

Who's early for lunch?
What's the waitress's name?
What is the waitress saying?
What looks marvelous?
What's Ms. Allen having for lunch?

PRACTICE 4

Listen and repeat:

Now answer these questions.

What time is it?
Who's having lunch?
Where are the olives?
What color are the olives?
What's in Mr. Clark's hand?
What does Mr. Clark want?

DIALOGUE

Early for Lunch

Mr. Clark: Hello, Lily.
Waitress: Hello, Mr. Clark. You're early for lunch. It's only eleven o'clock.
Mr. Clark: When I come later, there's usually nothing left.
Waitress: What would you like today?
Mr. Clark: I'll have the leg of lamb.
Waitress: And would you like salad? The salad plate today is lettuce,
              tomatoes, and black olives.
Mr. Clark: Marvelous! I love olives.
Waitress: And what would you like to drink?
Mr. Clark: A glass of lemonade, please. And a slice of melon for dessert.
Waitress: Would you like the lemonade now?
Mr. Clark: Later, thanks, Lily – with the lamb.

UNIT 44

l • ball
Part 2

voice

The *l* in these words often has a slightly different sound.

PRACTICE 1

Listen and repeat:

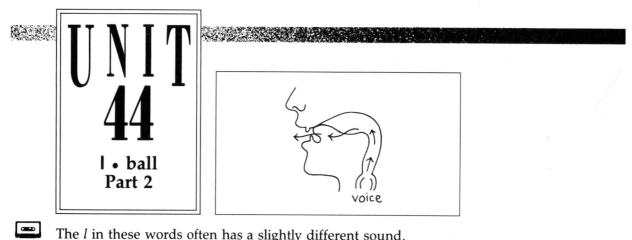

	Sound 1	*Sound 2*
10	ten	tell
pin	pin	pill
bone	bone	bowl

TEST

Listen to these sentences. Circle the word in parentheses that you hear.

1. I dropped a (pin/pill).
2. That's the dog's (bone/bowl).
3. Was he (in/ill)?

PRACTICE 2

Listen and repeat:

beautiful	bicycle	pull	spoiled
careful	little	difficult	holding
sensible	gentleman	myself	child
special	Paul	help	always
uncle	fall	fault	salesperson
Michael	I'll		

DIALOGUE

A Spoiled Little Boy

(Michael and his Uncle Paul visit a bicycle store.)

Michael: What a beautiful bicycle!
Uncle Paul: Michael! Be careful!
Salesperson: Excuse me, please. This child is too little to ride this bicycle. It's a very difficult bicycle to . . .
Uncle Paul: Be careful, Michael!
Michael: You're always telling me to be careful. I don't need help. I won't fall.
Salesperson: But, sir. This is a special bicycle. It's . . .
Michael: Don't pull the bicycle, Uncle Paul. I'll do it myself.
Uncle Paul: Be sensible, Michael. This gentleman says it's . . . *(Michael falls.)*
Michael: It was Uncle Paul's fault. He was holding the bicycle.

INTONATION

Listen and repeat:

What a **won**derful **meal**!

Wonderful? You think it's **won**derful?

What a **dull film**!

Dull? You think it's **dull**?

CONVERSATION

Practice in pairs. Talk about the pictures. Use the adjectives below.

Example: bottle
    A: What an unusual bottle!
    B: Unusual? You think it's unusual?

wonderful   un**com**fortable   **little**   **small**
beautiful   **mis**erable   **dif**ficult   unu**su**al
horrible   **dull**   **sim**ple   **old**

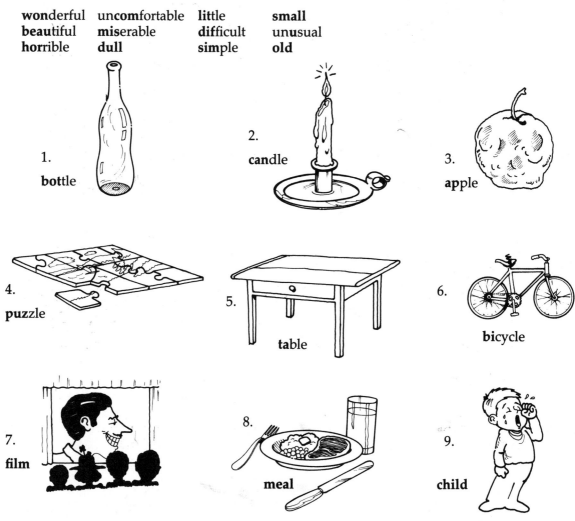

1. **bot**tle

2. **can**dle

3. **ap**ple

4. **puz**zle

5. **table**

6. **bicycle**

7. **film**

8. **meal**

9. **child**

SPELLING

The sound l is spelled with the letter *l*:

> *l*   late, lunch, glass, complain, always, unusual, wonderful, travel, pencil, told, fault
> whole, mile, bicycle, little, people, horrible, puzzle

> *ll*   small, fall, dull, spell, really, follow
> careful – carefully, control – controlling

The letter *l* is silent in:

> could, should, would, talk, chalk, walk, yolk, half, calf, salmon, calm,* palm*

*Some people pronounce the l in *calm* and *palm*.

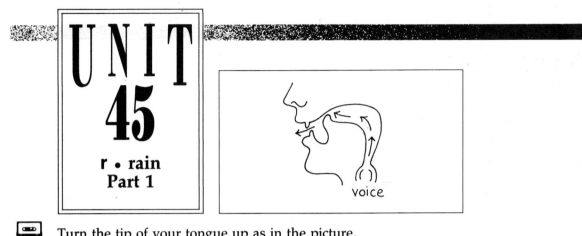

UNIT 45

r • rain
Part 1

Turn the tip of your tongue up as in the picture.
Do not touch the roof of your mouth with the tip of your tongue.
The sides of your tongue should touch your back teeth.

PRACTICE 1

Listen and repeat:

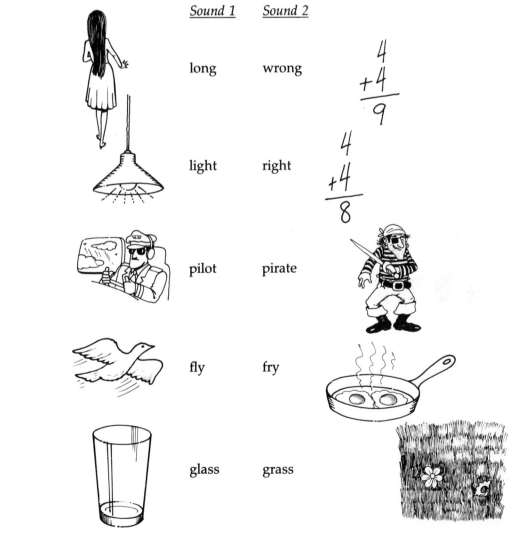

	Sound 1	*Sound 2*	
	long	wrong	
	light	right	
	pilot	pirate	
	fly	fry	
	glass	grass	

TEST

Listen to these sentences. Circle the word in parentheses that you hear.

1. That sentence is (long/wrong).
2. I'm going to (collect/correct) the homework.
3. Don't walk on the (glass/grass).
4. He was a famous (pilot/pirate).
5. Are you carrying the (light/right) suitcase?

PRACTICE 2

Listen and repeat:

Rose	very	programmer	waitress
reading	Maria	bright	interesting
restaurant	married	Chris	photographer
Rita	parent	grown up	truck
Rocky	proud	France	drives
reporter	pretty	country	secretary

PRACTICE 3

Listen and repeat:

really	Laura
Larry	library
children	librarian
Colorado	electrician

DIALOGUE

A Proud Parent

Maria: Are the children all grown up now, Rose?
Rose: Oh, yes. Laura's the oldest. She's a computer programmer.
Maria: Oh, very interesting. And what about Rita? She was such a bright child – always reading.
Rose: She's a librarian at the public library.
Maria: Really? And Chris? She was a very pretty little girl.
Rose: Chris is working as a waitress at a restaurant in Paris. She's married to a French photographer.
Maria: Oh, how interesting. And what about Larry and Rocky?
Rose: Larry drives a truck. He drives all over the country. We hardly ever see him.
Maria: Really? Where does he live now?
Rose: Colorado.
Maria: And does Rocky drive a truck, too?
Rose: Oh, no. Rocky is a pilot.
Maria: Really? Where does he fly to? Does he fly to other countries?
Rose: Yes. Mostly to England and France.

CONVERSATION

Ask somebody questions about Rose's children. Use the names and occupations below in your questions.

Examples:

    A: Is Laura a secretary?
    B: No, she isn't. She's a computer programmer.
    A: Is Rocky a reporter?
    B: No, he isn't. He's a pilot.

    Rocky   Laura   Chris   Larry   Rita   Chris's husband

    secretary   electrician   receptionist   librarian   reporter
    truck driver   pilot   writer   actress   psychologist

SPELLING

The sound r is usually written with the letter *r:*

    r   right, repeat, really, reporter, drive, proud, secretary
    rr   sorry, carry, tomorrow, correct, mirror, arrive

Other spellings:

    wr   wrong, write, wrist
    rh   rhyme, rhythm

UNIT
46
r • here
Part 2

When the sound r comes after a vowel, it often affects the way the vowel is pronounced.

PRACTICE 1

Listen and repeat:

	Sound 1	_Sound 2_	
	heel	hear	
	tail	tear	
	fall	four	
	file	fire	
	towel	tower	

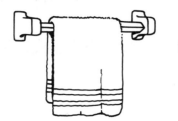

PRACTICE 2 📼

Listen and repeat:

	Sound 1	Sound 2
	cheese	cheers
	his	hears
	days	dares
	dead	dared
2 2	two's	tours

TEST

Listen to these sentences. Circle the word in parentheses that you hear.

1. Put these papers in the (file/fire).
2. (Fall/Four) is the best time to go there.
3. We liked the old (towels/towers) in Europe.
4. Could you move the (cot/cart), please?
5. The speech was followed by (cheese/cheers).
6. The restaurant seated the (two's/tours) first.

PRACTICE 3 🔲

Listen and repeat:

here	there	depart	early	more	tour	hours	tired
near	where	departure	clerk	four	sure	Howard	
clearly	care	supermarket	thirty	storm	Europe		
Leary	airport			important	Curie		
cafeteria	upstairs						
souvenir	everywhere						

DIALOGUE 🔲

At the Airport

ARRIVAL – DEPARTURE		
FLIGHT NUMBER	SCHEDULED DEPARTURE	ACTUAL DEPARTURE
444	12:30	4:34

Announcement: (*not very clear*) Attention, passengers on the 12:30 plane to New York. There will be a short delay. That flight will now depart at 4:34. Passengers should remain here at the airport. We are sorry . . .

Mrs. Leary: Did you hear that? Why can't they speak more clearly?

Ms. Curie: There's going to be a short delay. We're leaving at 4:34.

Mrs. Leary: SHORT delay?! That's four hours!

Dr. Howard: 4:34?! Oh, no! I have a very important meeting early tomorrow morning in New York. I'll never get there on time!

Mr. Leary: Is there a cafeteria here?

Ms. Curie: Yes. There's a cafeteria upstairs.

Mr. Leary: I'm going upstairs then. Coming, dear?

Mrs. Leary: No. I'll stay here. I'm so tired. We've been on a tour of Europe.

Ms. Curie: Oh! Where were you?

Mrs. Leary: Everywhere. Oh, dear. Four more hours at the airport . . .

Ms. Curie: Well, I'm going downstairs. There's a bookstore there and a souvenir store. There's even a supermarket. This is a marvelous airport!

Dr. Howard:	I don't care how marvelous the airport is. I have to get to New York. Oh! Here's an airline clerk. Excuse me. Is there a problem?
Airline clerk:	Oh, no, sir. There's a storm moving toward here. But it will be over in a couple of hours.
Dr. Howard:	Are you sure?
Airline clerk:	Oh, yes, sir. Our departure time is 4:34.

PRACTICE 4

Listen and repeat:

Excuse me. Is there a cafe**te**ria **near here**?
Yes. There's a cafe**te**ria over **there** on the **cor**ner.
Excuse me. Is there a **tour**ist **of**fice **near here**?
Sorry. I'm **really not sure**.

CONVERSATION

Ask other students in the class for directions to places in your town or neighborhood.

Example:
A: Excuse me. Is there a bookstore near here?
B: Yes. There's a bookstore on the corner.

A: Ask for things like these:

cafeteria	supermarket
airport	department store
park	flower store
tourist office	hardware store
barber	souvenir store
hairdresser	fire alarm

B: Give answers like these:

Yes. Right over there.
Yes. There's a . . . | downstairs.
                      | upstairs.
                      | near the . . .
                      | on the corner.
Sorry. I'm really not sure.

SPELLING

ɪ/iy before r:
ear   near, hear, clearly, dear, ear, beard
eer   cheerful, career, deer
ere   here, atmosphere, we're
ier   cashier, pier
er   cafeteria, material, serious, experience
ir   souvenir

ε/ey before r:

are	care, scared, compare, prepare, square
air	airport, repair, upstairs, hair, chair
ere	where, there
ear	wear, pear, tear (verb), bear
eir	their
er(r)	very, terrible, cherry
ar(r)	Mary, Paris, parent, area, carry, marry

ʊ/uw before r:

ure	sure, pure, cure, mature
ur	curious, plural, Europe
our	tour
oor	poor

Note: Different speakers may pronounce some of these words differently.

Fanshawe College

London, Ontario

Acknowledgments

Pronunciation Pairs is based on the British text *Ship or Sheep?* by Ann Baker.

Illustrations were rendered by Kevin Callahan.
Mouth illustrations for unit opening pages 4, 6, 10, 12, 16, 20, 24, 26, 28, 32, 36, 38, 41, 46, 50, 52, 60, 86, 89, 93, 96, 112, 115, 126, 131, 132, 140, 142, 145 as well as illustrations on pages 2, 3, 66, 67 were rendered by Daisy de Puthod.

Text and cover designs are by Michael Pilla.

The Cassette set was produced by Phyllis Dolgin.